D0982412

ADIRONDACK 102 CLUB:
Your Passport & Guide to the North Country

Martin Podskoch, Editor

David Hayden, Asst. Editor

Contributors:

Adcock, Frederick & Cynthia
Aird, Leona
Alexander, Olive
Allen, Hector
Barton, Brenda
Blades, David
Boeye, Nancy
Boisen, Sharon
Brooks, Eleanor
Brunell, John
Bruno, Ron
Bryant Tim
Bunke, Charles
Burns, Michelle
Caldwell, Ted
Cameron, Cynthia
Canon, George H.
Carroll, Dee
Chase, William H.
Cianfarano, Dr. Stan
Clothier, Rachel
Converse, Mary
Cornell, Gordon
Couture, Jan
Cramer, Gail
Dandaraw, Ed
Danforth, Hilda

Darling, Eliza
Davis, Shelly
DeFayette, Melanie
Douglas, Randall
Edwards, Priscilla L.
Edwardsen, Roy
Eickhoff, Dennis E.
Evens, Bea
Farber, Bill
Feulner, Ron
Frasier, Evelyn
Friden, Mark
Gates, Sandra
Glebus, Gary
Glushko, Peter
Goodwin, Tony
Granger, Persis "Perky"
Greely, Eileen
Greenley-Hackel, Carol A.
Grunel, John
Haley, Teresa Brannon
Hall, Mark
Hammecker, Susan
Harrington, Charles
Hayes, Christine
Haynes, Letty
Healy, Joy

Hest, Robert
Hill, Patricia
Hoffman, Beverly
Homer, Patricia
Hotaling, Mary
Huck, Michelle
Huntington, Kathy
Johnson, Paula
Keough, Ronald
Kopp, Jon
Lagoy, Donna
Lee, Mitch
Light, Peter
Lord, Lansing
Mannix, Margaret
McGill, Joe
McDonough, Pat
McGowan, Mary
Nilsen, Richard
Nitto, Sue
Parisi, Steve
Pascucci, Sandy
Peabody, Charlotte & Allen
Peters, Karen
Parrott, Virginia
Pivetta, Ves
Provoncha, Fred

Provoncha, Joe
Ransom, Kevin
Reid, Beverly
Rielly, Kimberly
Roalsvig, Alexandra
Roberts, Lauren
Rongeau, Rita
Rosenbarker, Roy
Ryan, Leland
Scott, Roby
Smith, Jo Ann
Smith, Sylvia
Spaeth, Maria
Stevenson, Alice
Sweeney, Jack & Mary
Thurston, Davina M.
Towers, Brian
Town of Webb Historic Association
Verner, Abbie
Walker, Carolyn
Wever, Judy
Willis, Pat
Wright, Arthur "Mo"
Young, Ross
Zullo, William R.

Podskoch PRESS

East Hampton, Connecticut

i

Adirondack 102 Club

Published by
Podskoch Press, LLC
43 O'Neill Lane
East Hampton, CT 06424

www.adirondack102club.com
podskoch@comcast.net
www.adirondackstories.com
www.cccstories.com
www.firetowerstories.com

ISBN 978-0-9794979-7-1
Manufactured in the United States of America

654321
Cover Photo by Jeri Wright
Design & Layout by Amanda Beauchemin of Ford Folios
Maps by Paul Hartmann

TABLE OF CONTENTS

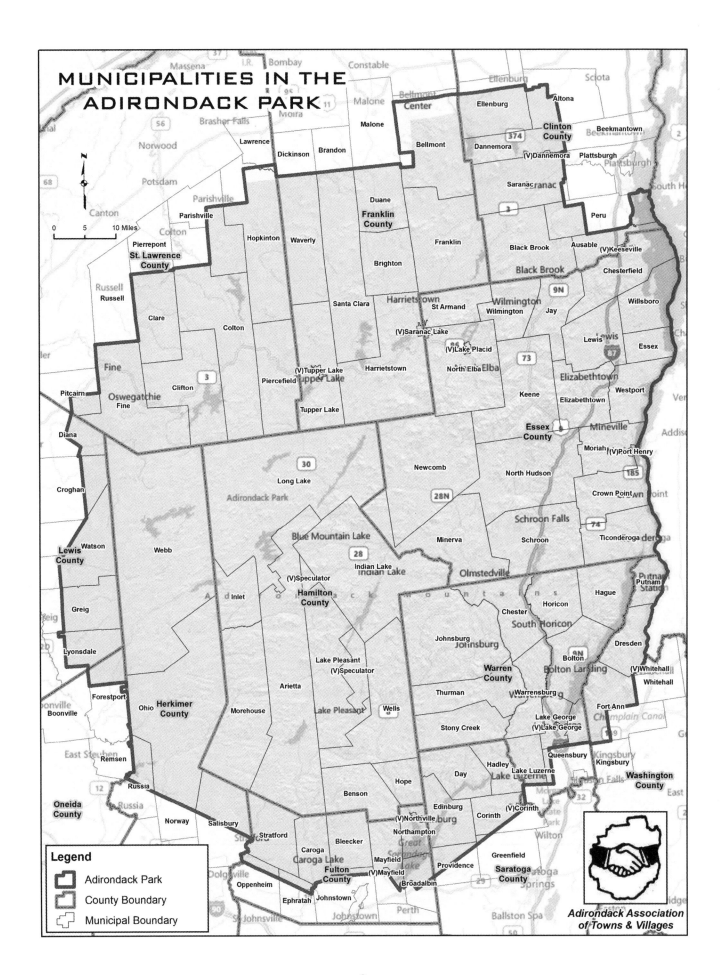

MUNICIPALITIES IN THE ADIRONDACK PARK

Legend
- Adirondack Park
- County Boundary
- Municipal Boundary

Adirondack Association of Towns & Villages

2

PREFACE

THIS BOOK is an invitation I encourage you to accept.

I have the incredible honor of representing much of the Adirondacks – a wonderful place in which to live and an unforgettable destination for millions of tourists who visit each year.

Nestled among our majestic mountains are 102 towns and villages – a string of unique communities that together tell the narrative of life today, and yesterday, in the Adirondacks.

My work as a New York State Senator has brought me to most of the communities described so well in this book. One of the most rewarding things about being a representative is the opportunity to meet so many different people. Each relationship is a chance to learn something new and I've learned a lot.

The "Adirondack 102 Club" is inspired in part by the early 20th Century Adirondack travels of Thomas Edison, Henry Ford, Harvey Firestone and John Burroughs – innovators whose shared pursuit of lifelong learning brought them together to the Adirondacks.

I hope you, too, are inspired to explore the Adirondacks and to learn something new and unexpected about our history, our traditions, our way of life and our future.

It is one thing to say "I visited the Adirondacks," but quite another to say "I experienced the Adirondacks." I promise an enriching journey and encourage you to do so with friends and loved ones with this unique passport in hand. A great adventure awaits!

Best Regards,
Senator Betty Little

INTRODUCTION

Since 2001, I have traveled to all of the 102 towns and villages in the Adirondacks gathering stories for my five Adirondack books on fire towers, Civilian Conservation Corps Camps, and illustrated Adirondack Stories. In my travels people have taken me in for the night and shared their home, food, and stories. I have gotten to meet so many wonderful people and seen so many interesting places that I want to share my experience of this marvelous region.

In the Dec. 11, 2005 issue of American Profile Magazine I read about the Vermont 251 Club that was started in 1954 when Dr. Arthur W. Peach suggested the idea of an informal group, the 251 Club, to veer off the beaten path and "to discover the secret and lovely places that main roads do not reveal." He felt that every part of the state had beauty, history, attractions, traditions, and interesting people.

I have found that most people who visit the Adirondacks just visit one particular area where they have a cottage, hiked, or camped, or they have rented a cabin, motel or hotel. They do not know the Adirondacks unless they visit all the towns and many of the side roads. For eight years I wondered if I might be able to duplicate in the Adirondacks what Dr. Peach did in Vermont.

Then in December 2013 I mentioned this idea to Clark Seaman the Long Lake Town Supervisor. He thought it was a great idea and that I should contact Brian Towers, the President of the Adirondack Association of Towns and Villages (AATV). I called him and he, too, liked the idea and invited me to speak to the AATV meeting on Dec. 9, 2013 in Lake George. I accepted his invitation and was a little nervous to see what their reaction would be.

At my presentation I proposed to write a book with descriptions of all the towns and villages highlighting their location, history, traditions, and interesting places to visit. I also asked the town supervisors if they would find someone in their town or village to write the description. This would be better than me writing about their town since I didn't know all of the history and interesting places. I also pointed out to the supervisors that the new club would also be an economic plus for the many small towns that are less visited.

I thought that once the request went out that I'd get replies in a month or two. After many calls and emails to entice someone to write about their town, I had all 102 town and village summaries completed in June, 2014. Most of the writers were the town historians but there were also town supervisors, assessors, chambers of commerce, historical societies, and residents who contributed. They all did a great job of writing and sent photos that would be used in the book and on the Adirondack 102 Club website.

Sallie Way, my sister-in-law and art teacher at Shenendehowa High School (Clifton Park, NY), suggested that I make the book like a passport where visitors would get their book stamped or signed by a resident in each town. She even designed a logo for the club.

This book will be a guide to the travelers in their quest to visit all 102 towns and villages. Members will also learn about the history and fascinating places in the Adirondacks. By getting their book signed or stamped by a resident, they will also get to know the friendly locals and be able to ask them questions such as where there is a good place to eat or an interesting local attraction? Hopefully they will thereby get to know the real Adirondacks.

There are no rules or requirements to be a member. No documents to turn in. One may keep a journal in addition to this book in their quest. There is no membership fee, just a desire to experience the whole Adirondack region. Adults and children of all ages can be members. What a great adventure for families, grandparents and their grandchildren or by themselves. Most members will travel by car while others might use a bike, motorcycle, walk, or maybe a canoe!

Once a member has reached their goal of all 102 towns & villages they will then receive the "Vagabond" award. I chose this name because there was a group of influential men who made trips in the Adirondacks and other parts of the US to get away from their busy lives and learn about nature.

"Vagabonds" is how Thomas Edison, Henry Ford, Harvey Firestone & John Burroughs described themselves when they took automobile camping trips together in the Adirondacks & other sojourns throughout America to get away from their busy lives. Each man contributed a skill. Edison was the "navigator," Ford the "mechanic," Firestone the "organizer" and Burroughs the "naturalist." A caravan of cars & trucks carried the "Vagabonds," workers, a cook, camping equipment & a chuck wagon. Ford organized contests, such as sprints, tree climbing, and tree chopping. After dinner they relaxed by the campfire discussing issues of the day. Each Vagabond had his own tent with electric lights. They traveled through the Adirondacks twice. In 1916 they camped near Saratoga Springs, Indian Lake, Elizabethtown, Au Sable Forks, Paul Smiths & Plattsburgh. In 1919 they picked their spots as the day allowed: Loon Lake, Long Lake, Lake Placid and Plattsburgh. They were the source of many news stories and their trips led NYS to build campsites to encourage auto camping.

So now begin your quest as a member of the Adirondack 102 Club to not only visit all the towns and villages but get to know the real Adirondacks. Let's all take the road less traveled!

– Marty Podskoch

5

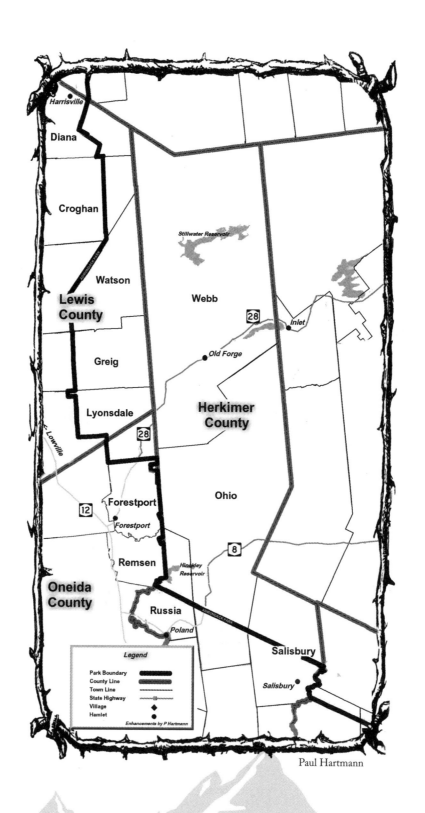

Harrisville

Diana

Croghan

Stillwater Reservoir

Watson

Lewis County

Webb

28

Inlet

Greig

Old Forge

Lyonsdale

Herkimer County

28

Forestport

12

Ohio

Forestport

8

Remsen

Hinckley Reservoir

Oneida County

Russia

Poland

Salisbury

Salisbury

Legend

Park Boundary	
County Line	
Town Line	
State Highway	
Village	◆
Hamlet	●

Enhancements by P Hartmann

Paul Hartmann

6

CHAPTER 1

REGION I:

HERKIMER, LEWIS & ONEIDA COUNTIES

CROGHAN

The Town of Croghan was organized April 5, 1841 from the Town of Diana and Town of Watson. Located in Lewis County, bounded by Herkimer County, Town of New Bremen, Town of Denmark, Town of Diana and Town of Wilna (located in Jefferson County).

The township was named after General George Croghan who became famous as a War of 1812 hero at the sieges of Fort Meigs and Fort Stephenson in Ohio. In 1848 a section of the town was taken to form part of the Town of New Bremen. The Town of Croghan was mainly settled by settlers from France, Germany, and Switzerland. Many families of these early settlers still reside here. Part of the Town of Croghan is located within the Adirondack Park.

Located within the town are the Village of Croghan (French Settlement), and the hamlets of Beaver Falls, Belfort, Indian River (Bent's Settlement), and Naumburg (Prussian Settlement). Forest City and Jerden Falls were once thriving hamlets but today are only a memory.

Tanneries, sawmills, logging, papermaking, and farming were the main industries in the early years using the natural resources. Today, the town's main industries are farming, maple syrup, logging, tourism, papermaking, and production of electricity on the Beaver River.

PLACES TO VISIT

Croghan Bologna began in 1888 and is famous for its bologna and sausage and smoked meats. 9824 Main St., Croghan.

Croghan Candy Kitchen offers delicious handmade candies. 9740 Main St., Croghan.

Good Ol' Wishy's Ice Cream Parlor is an old-fashioned soda fountain noted for its huge "Adirondack Sized Cone," milkshakes and sundaes. 9779 Main St., Croghan.

The American Maple Museum exhibits the history of maple syrup and sugar making techniques ranging from those used by the Native Americans to plastic tubing and stainless steel evaporators in use today. 9753 Main St., Croghan. www.americanmaplemuseum.org

Railroad Historical Society of Northern New York is a former railroad depot converted to a museum teeming with artifacts of life in the old days. 9784 Main St., Croghan.

There are many seasonal and year-round camps located in the town. The Beaver River and the West Branch of the Oswegatchie River flow through the town. The Black River and the Beaver River provide part of the southern border. There are many ponds, streams, wetlands, open fields, and forests located here. Beauty abounds through all four seasons.

Oswegatchie Educational Center is located on Long Pond and is a picturesque place to visit. www.oswegatchie.org

There are many activities to partake in, including visiting museums, hunting and fishing, riding snowmobiles/ATVs (you need to check roads before traveling), cross-country skiing, boating, and canoeing.

Material courtesy of Jack & Mary Sweeney, Town of Croghan Historians

DATE: _____ WEATHER: _____

MEMORIES: _____

_____

_____

_____

_____

_____

_____

_____

_____

_____

_____

_____

_____

_____

_____

[Passport Stamp / Signature Here]

In 1977 the American Maple Museum was founded with the purpose of preserving the history and evolution of the North American maple syrup industry. It is located in the former Father Leo Memorial School and is one of the treasures in the Town of Croghan. Jack & Mary Sweeney

9

DIANA

The Town of Diana is in the northeastern corner of Lewis County and part of its eastern section is in the Adirondack Park. It is composed of the Village of Harrisville, and these hamlets: Diana Center, Kimball Mill, Lake Bonaparte, Lewisburg, Natural Bridge, and Remington Corners.

The town was named after the Roman goddess of the hunt. She was associated with wild animals and woodland, and having the power to talk to and control animals.

If you are coming from the Watertown area heading northeast on Rt. 3 and travel 30 miles, you will reach the Town of Diana. Traveling a few miles on the left you will reach the Lake Bonaparte area that was named after Joseph Bonaparte, the brother of Napoleon. There are three roads leading to the Lake, South Shore, East Shore, and North Shore, all having views of the lake. The south shore has a Gazebo with area for public swimming, camping, and Ziggy's a swell restaurant/bar. The east shore is where the beautiful Hermitage Hotel once stood that burned in 1953. On that site there is now a restaurant/bar called the Phoenix with a view of the lake and a place to dock your boat. On the south shore you can dock a boat and there is rough camping on the state property.

As you leave Lake Bonaparte heading northeast on Rt. 3 you arrive in the Village of Harrisville. It was named after Foskit Harris who settled here in 1833; it was a thriving village in the late 1800s and early 1900s. There still are many things to see and do at the present time such as, the Town of Diana Historical Museum located in the old train depot that was built in 1887. Just past Stewarts, take a left on Maple Street, and before you cross the railroad tracks turn left

on Depot Street and you will see the Museum at 8203 Depot St. It's an interesting place to visit with numerous artifacts and pictures accompanying a history of the area, and also a gift shop. Open Memorial Day weekend thru Labor Day. Tuesday thru Saturday, 10 am – 3 pm. 315-543-1010

Backtrack to Rt. 3, and turn left and cross the bridge over the Oswegatchie River and make a right onto Main Street. Then turn left into Scenic View parking. As you look across the river you will see a Gazebo on the island within walking distance where you can have a picnic lunch or just enjoy the view.

In the area there are three places to eat: the bakery and two restaurants or have your ice cream at the Ice Cream Shop. There are also two quick-stops where you can get gas and a bite to eat.

As you leave Harrisville heading northeast on Rt. 3, you are going to be heading into the beautiful Adirondack Mountains.

Material courtesy of Ross Young,
Town of Diana

10

DATE: _____ WEATHER: _____

MEMORIES: _____

_____

_____

_____

_____

_____

_____

_____

_____

_____

_____

_____

_____

_____

[Passport Stamp / Signature Here]

The Town of Diana Historical Society is located at the old railroad station pictured above.
Ross Young

FORESTPORT

The Town of Forestport is located in the northeast corner of Oneida County and its northern part is in the Adirondack Park. The town is often laughingly referred to as "Punkeyville" after the small biting black flies. It includes the hamlets of Woodgate (formerly White Lake Corners), Forestport, Woodhull, and Forestport Station.

HISTORY

Forestport was originally Williamsville, renamed in 1870, and is the youngest town in Oneida County. The town was built around mills and tanneries on the rivers. When the Erie Canal was built in the 1850s and later the Black River Canal, a feeder canal was built to Forestport. The canals spurred settlement in the area. Reservoirs and dams were built. Water through the feeder became a way to market for the residents in the area for lumber, shingles, and products from the tanneries, along with their crops of potatoes and hops. The railroad was built in 1891 bringing more industry, a faster way to market, and summer visitors and sportsmen. In 1911 Woodgate also boasted the world's largest icehouse along the shores of White Lake, serving areas as far away as New York City. In 1945 the last logs were floated on waterways.

There is little industry left and the area is currently referred to as a vacation destination, at the entrance to the Adirondack Park, with people enjoying summer activities on the local lakes: Kayuta, Little Long Lake, White Lake, and Otter Lake. There are also many hiking trails through the Adirondack Park, and the area is a winter wonderland for snowmobilers, cross-country skiers, and snowshoers. It is also a favorite destination for viewing the spectacular fall foliage.

POINTS OF INTEREST

Buffalo Head Restaurant. 10626 N Lake Rd., Woodhull. 315-392-6607, www.buffaloheadrestaurant.com

Garramone's. 11770 O'Brien Rd., Woodhull. 315-392-2052, www.garramonesrestaurant.com

White Lake Inn. 12676 Rt. 28, Woodgate. 315-392-5439

Seasons Café. Rt. 28 & Bear Creek Rd., Woodgate. 315-392-6556

Kayuta Lake Campground. 10892 Campground Rd., Forestport. www.kayutalakecampground.com

Camp Russell is one of the oldest Boy Scouts camps in the US. It was founded in 1918 on White Lake. 12370 Rt. 28, Woodgate.

Masonic Camp and Camp Nazareth are located on Little Long Lake.

Woodgate Free Library has a large historical collection and is located at the intersection of Woodgate Drive and Rt. 28 in Woodgate. 315-392-4814, www.midyork.org/woodgate

Material courtesy of Sandy Pascucci, Woodgate Free Library

DATE: _____ WEATHER: _____

MEMORIES: _____

_____

_____

_____

_____

_____

_____

_____

_____

_____

_____

_____

_____

_____

[Passport Stamp / Signature Here]

The logging industry was very important in the early history of Forestport. Above, teams of horses are hauling pine logs in the winter. Woodgate Library Collection

GREIG

Located on the southeast corner of Lewis County Greig covers 292 square miles, two thirds located in the Adirondack Park. The town includes these hamlets: Greig, Bushes Landing, Petries Corners, Pine Grove, Sperryville, and part of Watson. There are also these lakes: Brantingham, Beaver, Francis, and Soft Maple Reservoir.

HISTORY

The town of Greig was formed from Watson in 1828 and was first known as Brantingham. The name was changed to Grieg in 1832. Since vast forests have always covered a large percentage of Greig, and because there are a number of streams and larger rivers running through, almost all the early industries were connected with logging and the making of wood products such as shingles, excelsior, broom handles, laths and toys. There were also tanneries and sawmills. Most often, these operations were situated on the waterways for convenience and for power. One typical tannery in Greig might process 50,000 hides of leather and use 4,600 cords of hemlock bark. Logging continues to be a fervent industry to this day. The soil is not good for raising agriculture, so farming was mostly practiced on a subsistence level. It was 1870 before Greig even had its own post office!

The first hotel on Brantingham Lake was built in 1873 and the lake became a recreational destination that continues to operate today, offering much for the outdoor enthusiast vacationer. There were two childrens' camps built to take advantage of the accessible woods and water, one of which, Aldersgate, remains and thrives today. 7955 Brantingham Rd., Greig. www.aldersgateny.org

POINTS OF INTEREST

Brantingham Lake area offers public boating, fishing, hunting, hiking, biking, ATV, horse, and snowmobile trails, the Brantingham Golf Club, Catspaw Country Market and a variety of restaurants including the Pine Tree Tavern, Brantingham Inn Motel, Trailside Inn, and Coach Light Inn.

Much of Greig's woods and water is located on private land and not accessible to the public. The exception to this are five lovely streams with waterfalls ideal for hiking, picnicking, and swimming.

Eatonville Falls is easily accessible on the Eatonville Rd. that runs off of the Pine Grove Rd. The falls and rocks to climb make a good place to hike and picnic. Access to the Independence River is on the northern border of the town at the end of the Donnattsburg Road. Here one can hike, swim, picnic, or take a tube down the river.

Shingle Mills Falls is located in the Brantingham Lake area approx. four miles down the Partridgeville Rd. on the left are the Shingle Mills Falls. Here in the Independence River Wild Forest is a one-mile easy walk that culminates at a wide 10-foot waterfall on the Otter Creek. Details about a hike to Gleasman Falls can be found at www.nnywaterfalls.com/independenceriver/gleasmanfalls.

Singing Waters Park is a 105-acre tract of reforested white pine. It is located just east of Rt. 12 between Lyons Falls and Glenfield. Take Burdick Crossing Rd. east to Lyons Falls Rd., Co. Rt. 39. Take a right here and then a left on Fish Creek Rd. The Singing Waters Park will be a short distance down on the left.

DATE: _____ WEATHER: _____

MEMORIES: _____

_____

_____

_____

_____

_____

_____

_____

_____

_____

_____

_____

_____

_____

[Passport Stamp / Signature Here]

For more information, visit:
www.branthingham.com
www.brantingham.org
www.lewiscountychamber.org

Material courtesy of Patricia Homer,
Town of Greig Historian

Independence River flows through the Town of Greig and is known for fine fishing. Patricia Homer

LYONSDALE

The Town of Lyonsdale is in the southeast corner of Lewis County in the southwestern part of the Adirondack Park. It is approximately 18 miles south of Lowville on Rt. 12. The town includes the villages of Lyons Falls and part of Port Leyden and the hamlet of Lyonsdale.

Lyonsdale was first settled in the late 1700s and was named after Caleb Lyon. He and his wife, Marietta Dupont, arrived in 1819. Caleb was a land agent who attracted many settlers to the area. He built a bridge across the Moose River and several mills. Lyons Falls was the home of the large Gould Paper Mill (est. 1895) at the junction of the Black and Moose rivers. It closed in 2000. Lyonsdale still depends on forest products such as wood pulp for its economy.

The Moose River flows through the town and has some of the best kayaking in the NE. The lower Moose River is considered Class 5 whitewater. In the spring, you can view the whitewater kayakers coming over the falls. Fortis US, a hydroelectric power plant, maintains a recreational area at Agers Falls. There is parking, picnic tables and grills, an historical pavilion, and a hiking trail along the Moose River. It also has a boat launch and swimming. From Lyons Falls, take Co. Rt. 39 across the Black River. Veer left onto Lyonsdale Rd., which is still Co. Rt. 39, and drive about 2 mi. to the entrance on the left.

According to the "Classic Northeastern Whitewater Guide" published by Appalachian Mountain Club Books, the Lower Moose provides a run appropriate for intermediate to advanced paddlers. Water is generally reliable from April through mid-June and Columbus Day weekend through the end of October. The

Lower Moose has several drops of 20 feet and some that are easily 40 feet or more.

Lyonsdale is located on the Northern Tier Bicycle Route that goes from Anacortes, Washington to Bar Harbor, Maine.

The Storms-Bailey Home Museum located at 6929 Laura Street is a small home showcasing the 1940s and can be seen by appointment by calling 315-348-8379.

Lyons Falls Library is located in the beautiful Carriage House of the Gould Mansion. 3918 High St., Lyons Falls.

Riverside Park on Laura Street is where the Moose and Black rivers meet. It has an exercise trail with equipment, a boat/canoe launch, a hiking trail, bathrooms, picnic tables, a playground, tennis courts, a skating rink. There is also a Farmer's Market every Tuesday from June thru October, 12 Noon – 6 pm, and lunch is available there. Several restaurants and small businesses are also close by.

This is truly a four-season recreational area with beautiful vistas and two rivers in which to swim, paddle, or fish. In the winter there is plenty of snow for cross-country skiing, snowshoeing, and snowmobiling.

Lyonsdale is a quiet, unhurried, and friendly place. Come play in our beautiful little corner of the Adirondacks.

Material courtesy of Susan Hammecker, Lyons Falls History Association

DATE: _____ WEATHER: _____

MEMORIES: _____

_____

_____

_____

_____

_____

_____

_____

_____

_____

_____

_____

_____

_____

_____

_____

[Passport Stamp / Signature Here]

A kayaker navigating the Moose River. Joe Hammecker

17

OHIO

The Town of Ohio is located in the scenic foothills of the southwestern Adirondack Park at the center of Herkimer County. It is approx. 22 miles northeast of Utica and approx. 12 miles east of Boonville. The town includes these hamlets: Ohio, Atwell, Bull Hill, Gray, North Wilmurt, Nobleboro, and Wilmurt Corners. These lakes are in the town: Honnedaga, Limekiln, North, and South.

Ohio is drained by the Black and West Canada creeks and their tributaries. The soil is a sandy loam with some clay and well-suited for grazing.

One of the early settlers was the Mount family who were among 94 persons that came to the region on the Jerseyfield Patent. They cleared the land and began farming. During the American Revolution some settlers were killed by the Indians. After the war more settlers arrived. A sawmill and tannery were established in Grayville in the 1840s. During the 1800s farming was an important industry. In 1875 the records for dairy products included 79,800 pounds of cheese and 42,075 pounds of butter from 1,049 cows. 186 swine were slaughtered producing 46,737 pounds of pork. Lumbering was also an important industry in the 1800s with sawmills along the many streams.

The Town of Ohio was formerly the Town of West Brunswick. It was taken from the Town of Norway and named West Brunswick on April 11, 1823. In 1836 it was changed to the Town of Ohio and named after the state.

In the same year a portion of the town was taken off and annexed to the Town of Wilmurt. The Town of Ohio was located within the Jerseyfield Patent, except the

portion lying northwest of the West Canada Creek, which was in the Remsenburg Patent. Later in 1918 Wilmurt was reincorporated into the Town of Ohio.

The population in 1865 was 928 according to the Gazetteer & Business Directory of Herkimer County. In 2010 the population was 1,002 according to the Federal Census Records.

RECREATION

There are many streams and several lakes in the Town of Ohio that are great for fishing, boating, tubing, and kayaking.

West Canada Creek runs through Ohio and empties into Hinkley Reservoir. It then continues to the Mohawk River at Herkimer. The West Canada Creek is well-known for its native brook trout.

The Southern Adirondack Trail (SAT) travels through the Town of Ohio. The SAT carries travelers from Herkimer and Little Falls, past mountains and lakes and into Adirondack hamlets. Hiking, boating, cycling, and fishing are just a sample of the outdoor activities available along the trail. There is a parking area on Rt. 8, with picnic benches at mile marker 8/2308/1136.

Ice skate at Ohio Town Park Pavilion (winter).

Outdoor Fitness Trail in the Town Park.

Ohio Ridge Riders Club: This snowmobile club has a "Snow Bash," snowmobile grass drags (in September when there is no snow), and a snow show. www.ohioridgeriders.com

Adirondack Park & Forest Preserve Scenic View Parking Area is located in Noblesboro on

18

DATE: _____ WEATHER: _____

MEMORIES: _____

_____

_____

_____

_____

_____

_____

_____

_____

_____

_____

_____

_____

_____

[Passport Stamp / Signature Here]

Haskell Rd. off Rt. 8, just before mile marker 8/2308/1199. It is the gateway to the great North Woods and is in the West Canada Creek Watershed. The West Canada Creek is classified and protected under the New York State Wild, Scenic and Recreational Rivers System Act.

Material courtesy of Sandra Gates, Town of Ohio Historian

The Ohio Tavern and Restaurant has a long history of serving homemade food in the Town of Ohio. It also hosts drag races on its property in the winter. Scott Bagetis

19

REMSEN

Nestled in the foothills of the southwestern Adirondacks just off Rt. 12 is the small community of Remsen. It is in the northeastern section of Oneida County and its population in 2010 was 1,929. It includes the Village of Remsen (population 508).

The Town of Remsen was formed from the Town of Norway in 1798. Many of Remsen's first settlers were from Wales. Today the craftsmanship of those early Welsh residents is visible in the many historic buildings.

In 1908 the cornerstone was laid for the Didymus Thomas Library located at 9639 Main Street. The exterior of this beautiful library is made of pressed yellow brick and marble while the interior's special features include a balcony and majestic pillars all finished in oak.

Capel Cerrig or Stone Church located at 9793 Prospect St. is another treasure, built in 1831. Today this church, known as Stone Meeting House, is owned by Remsen Steuben Historical Society and is listed on the National Register of Historic Places.

Trains once played an important role in Remsen. In 1997 local volunteers began to rebuild the depot on its original foundation. Today it's a flag stop for the Adirondack Scenic Railroad. The Train Depot, located on Depot Street, is a multi-functional facility. One of its main attractions each fall is their corn maze.

The Remsen Baptist Church built in 1893 is located at 9627 Main St. Today it's known as the Remsen Performing and Visual Arts Center and it hosts many events including concerts, classes, programs and shows. A village walking tour map is available at the Remsen Arts Center.

Remsen is a destination for outdoor enthusiasts. The town is bordered by two lakes, Kayuta and Hinckley. The lakes offer activities such as boating, fishing, swimming, kayaking, and camping. During the winter, visitors use the area trails for cross-country skiing, snowshoeing and snowmobiling. Cincinnati Creek with its natural fall of about 20 feet on the south end of the village attracts kayakers during high waters.

If you're looking for a fun restaurant, try the Soda Fountain at 9698 Main St., Remsen. The main dining room is stylized in 1950s decor, viz. black & white checkered floor, sparkling red & silver vinyl seating, boomerang table tops, neon lights, and a Juke Box!

Remsen Barn Festival of the Arts began in 1980 and is held the fourth full weekend in September. Hundreds of vendors line Main Street with booths offering handmade crafts, produce and great food. Barn Fest attracts thousands of people to Remsen. It's a great time to visit!

Remsen is proud of both its historic past and our present native Olympian, Erin Hamlin. In 2014 she won a bronze medal in Luge at Sochi, Russia. Way to go Erin!

Material courtesy of Patricia Hill, Town of Remsen Historian

DATE: _____ WEATHER: _____

MEMORIES: _____

_____

_____

_____

_____

_____

_____

_____

_____

_____

_____

_____

_____

_____

_____

[Passport Stamp / Signature Here]

An early 1900 Henry M. Beach postcard depicts the Didymus Thomas Library, the old 1831 stone church, and train depot. Patricia Hill

RUSSIA

The Town of Russia is in the west central part of Herkimer County 16 miles north of Herkimer. The northern part of the town is in the Adirondack Park and the town includes the villages of Poland and Cold Brook.

The Town of Russia was first formed from the Town of Norway on April 7, 1806 and was called Union; it was renamed Russia in April, 1808 for unknown reasons.

Permanent settlement of the area began after the Revolutionary War when early arrivals were attracted by the water power along the West Canada and Cold Brook streams. The Village of Poland was settled about 1800 but not incorporated until 1890.

The Village of Cold Brook was settled after 1790 but was bustling with industry by the early 1800s because of the availability of water power produced by the Cold Brook stream.

There are also several picturesque hamlets that promote Russia's small town friendly atmosphere: Gravesville, Grant, Wheelertown, Trenton Falls, and Russia Corners. The latter is a historic district consisting of four houses, a church, and a schoolhouse.

The Russia Union Church (1820) is only open for special services and tours but the Cold Brook Methodist Church, located at 467 Main St., Rt. 8, has an active congregation with weekly services.

RECREATION

Hinckley Lake is a six-mile by one-and-a-half mile reservoir formed by damming the West Canada Creek in 1911. Both the lake and creek are a major waterway that forms the western boundary of the town. The West Canada is considered by many to be one of the best trout fishing streams in the state. Recreational campsites are situated along the West Canada Creek throughout the Kuyahoora Valley.

Trail's End Campground offers trails, boating, fishing, camping, and much more next to Hinckley Reservoir (438 MacArthur Rd., Cold Brook). People also use the creek for tubing, canoeing, and kayaking.

Hunting and trapping are also favorite pastimes. Many types of wildlife may be observed throughout the town.

During the winter months residents and visitors cross-country ski, ice skate, sled, or follow the many well-kept snowmobile trails.

Kuyahoora Town Park located behind the Poland Elementary School in Cold Brook, offers hiking and nature trails, baseball and soccer fields, a basketball court, a skateboarding park, pavilions, a playground, and a summer recreation program. Tennis courts are available at Poland School.

Geocaching is also popular with several spots throughout the town for participants to find using their GPS receiver or mobile device and other navigational techniques to hide and seek containers.

Shawangunk Nature Preserve is a 345-acre Forever Wild Nonprofit Deep Ecology Learning and Cultural Center that offers a variety of workshops and concerts throughout the year. The public is welcome to walk trails, borrow bicycles, observe the over 30 different bird species, visit the Nature Library, or use the preserve's canoes any time from May to December. 255 Shawangunk Rd., Cold Brook.

DATE: _____ WEATHER: _____

MEMORIES: _____

_____

_____

_____

_____

_____

_____

_____

_____

_____

_____

_____

_____

[Passport Stamp / Signature Here]

Historic Trenton Falls is open to the public twice a year; once in the spring and once in the fall. Tours are offered from 9 am – 5 pm on these dates. Directions from Utica: Take Rt. 12 North into Mapledale commercial district. Go past traffic light & take the next right onto Rt. 28 south. Follow to first left on curve, which is Trenton Falls Rd. Follow signs to four way stop. Go straight through and continue to the end of the road where you can park. For this year's tour dates, visit: town.trenton.ny.us.

A scenic view of Historic Trenton Falls. Paula Johnson

Material courtesy of Paula Johnson, Town of Russia Historian

23

SALISBURY

The Town of Salisbury is in the southeastern section of Herkimer County and the northern part of town is in the Adirondack Park. It is north of Little Falls and includes the hamlets of Salisbury, Curtis, Salisbury Center, Irondale, Ives Hollow, and Paper Mill.

On March 3, 1797 Salisbury was organized into a town. It wasn't until 20 years later, April 7, 1817 that it was annexed to Herkimer County. Immigration into the area began around 1794 because of two very valuable resources, acres of virgin timber and Spruce Creek which was a natural source of water power for mill wheels.

Several industries were established along the Spruce Creek including gristmills, carding mills, dressing mills, tanneries, sawmills, and a peg mill. Blacksmith shops, hotels, taverns, churches, cheese factories, and 14 one-room school houses were eventually built.

The land contained high quality black magnetic ore (magnetite) and by 1865 loads of iron ore were hauled daily. The mines closed for a time but reopened by William H. Switzer and the Salisbury Steel & Iron Company quickly amassed an empire. A famous 20-room mansion was built and a logging railroad which joined at Salisbury Center and ran through the woods to Jerseyfield Lake.

HISTORIC PLACES

Salisbury Covered Bridge: At one time there were seven covered bridges in Salisbury spanning Spruce Creek. Today the Salisbury Covered Bridge is the only one remaining in Herkimer County. It's located in Salisbury Center on the Fairview Road near the intersection of Rts. 29 and 29A. It's been renovated and is listed on the National Register of Historic Places. It was built in 1875 by Alvah Hopson on the lawn of his home and then transported to its present location. It was constructed of multiple king posts and Burr arch truss styles with large wooden pegs. It is a single span of nearly 50' in length. While visiting Salisbury bring a picnic lunch and enjoy the beauty of the Salisbury Covered Bridge. Spruce Creek is also great for fishing. Within walking distance is the Frisbie House.

Frisbie House was built in 1805 for Augustus Frisbie. It was the first framed house in Salisbury Center. The Salisbury Historical Society purchased and restored the house. Here you will see historical artifacts, town replicas, and historical exhibits. Tours are only by appointment by contacting the Town Clerk at 315-429-8581. The Frisbie House, located at 109 Rt. 29A in Salisbury Center, is on the National Register of Historic Places, as well as the Salisbury Center Grange No. 624, located on Rt. 29, Salisbury Center.

Salisbury Ridge Runners: This snowmobile organization, located in Salisbury Corners, is the largest snowmobile club in NYS with over 140 miles of well-maintained trails. www.salisburyridgerunners.com

Material courtesy of Brenda Barton, Town of Salisbury Historian

DATE: _____ WEATHER: _____

MEMORIES: _____

_____

_____

_____

_____

_____

_____

_____

_____

_____

_____

_____

_____

_____

[Passport Stamp / Signature Here]

The restored 1873 Covered Bridge is located in Salisbury Center on the Fairview Road near the intersection of Rts. 29 and 29A. Brenda Barton

WATSON

The Town of Watson is in eastern Lewis County. The eastern part of the town is in the western part of the Adirondack Park. The town is approx. 10 miles east of Lowville. In 2010 the population was 1,881. The town includes these hamlets: Bushes Landing, Eagle Falls, Moshier Falls, Number Four, Petries Corners, Pine Grove, Sperryville, and Watson and these lakes Beaver Lake, Chase Lake, Francis Lake, and Soft Maple Reservoir.

HISTORY

For several years before Watson was incorporated, Isaac Puffer and family were its only inhabitants. Puffer tried farming, built a sawmill near Chase Lake, and was accidentally shot by a friend in 1837.

Watson was named after James T. Watson who owned over 60,000 acres in Lewis and Herkimer counties. He was a wealthy merchant serving several important offices in New York State and died in 1808. His only son spent summers in Watson and committed suicide with a razor in 1839 at the age of 50. The Town of Watson was formed from Leyden in 1821. There were 44 families when the town was formed. At this time Watson embraced all of Lewis County east of the Black River.

In 1839 James Ranney's home was invaded by a panther that snatched his year old baby. It exited through a window with the baby but miraculously the child was not seriously injured.

There has never been a great deal of industry in the town except for lumbering and sawmilling. The sandy soil is not good for farming but potatoes were grown when the Black River Canal was operated and large amounts of

potatoes were shipped to city markets. There were also several cheese factories. Limburger cheese was still being made in the 1930s at Petries Corner. Between 1870 and 1960 there were many sawmills as well as a hemlock extract plant near Chase Lake. Sand and gravel operations continue to exist.

There were many camps and resorts. The Fenton House (1826) on the Number Four Rd. drew many tourists. A Boys Camp on Beaver Lake (1946) is now a popular Mennonite Christian Camp. Chase Lake was also a popular resort.

POINTS OF INTEREST

Historic Sites:
The Black River Canal Locks are off the Number Four Rd. across from Miller's Store in Watson. Also, Pine Grove Community Church (est. 1896) on Pine Grove Rd. is worth seeing because of its unusual interior construction.

The hamlet of Beache's Bridge and the hamlet of Petries Corner cemeteries on the Number Four Rd. Also there is one on Sperryville Rd. in the hamlet of Sperryville.

Recreation:
There are many horse and hiking trails. Canoeing and fishing is also popular at the lakes and rivers, especially the Black River.

Otter Creek Horse Trail System boasts 65 miles of horse trails and a campsite. Take Rt. 12 to Glenfield. Turn into the hamlet of Glenfield then turn east onto Greig Rd. Go across the Black River and in approx. 1.9 miles the road will make a T-connection with Pine Grove Rd. Turn left. Proceed 1.2 miles and take a right onto Chases Lake Rd. The entrance to the trailhead parking will be

DATE: _____ WEATHER: _____

MEMORIES: _____

_____

_____

_____

_____

_____

_____

_____

_____

_____

_____

_____

_____

[Passport Stamp / Signature Here]

approx. 3.4 miles on the right side of the road.

Watson's East Triangle Wild Forest provides fishing, hunting, and snowmobiling.

Material courtesy of Charles Bunke, Town of Watson Historian

In 2001 the Pine Grove Community Church Preservation Society, Inc. acquired the deed to the 1896 church on Pine Grove Rd. in Pine Grove. The Society's goal is to preserve it as a non-denominational facility accessible to the general public. www.townofwatsonny.com

27

WEBB

The Town of Webb, located in the central Adirondacks, is the largest township in New York State. It includes the hamlets of McKeever, Okara Lakes, Thendara, Old Forge, Eagle Bay, Big Moose, Stillwater, and Beaver River.

The youngest town in the Herkimer County, Webb was named for Dr. William Seward Webb, builder of the Mohawk and Malone Railroad through the region in 1892. The impact of the railroad upon the region was immediate. Thousands of people poured into the mountains to enjoy recreational and health-generating opportunities. Steamboats and guide boats brought them to the new hotels and guest houses along the lakes. Logging camps and mills provided jobs but claimed a fair share of the surrounding forests. Two decades of prosperity followed along with a great building boom. The jubilant citizens of the new township were unaware of the perils looming ahead in the new century, catastrophic forest fires, the decimation of forest lands and wildlife, and spiraling land prices.

Tourism drives the economy in the Town of Webb. It is still a land of rugged mountains with nearly 200 sparkling lakes and ponds. Approx. 1,900 year-round residents live in the small hamlets and along the waterways. Thousands more visit the region to enjoy boating, hiking, river rafting, skiing, snowmobiling, or to spend time with their families at their seasonal camp properties.

Old Forge and the Central Adirondack Region offers much for the vacationer during all seasons. Summer activities include boating, golf, water skiing, fishing, canoeing, hiking, swimming, and mountain biking.

POINTS OF INTEREST

Recreation:
McCauley Mountain. Skiing and snowmobiling, and when the snow is gone, ride the scenic chairlift and explore our hiking and biking trails on New York's Best Family Mountain. McCauley Rd., Old Forge.

Enchanted Forest Water Safari. Amusement rides and water park. Lodging available. 3183 Rt. 28, Old Forge.

Old Forge Lake Cruises. Narrated steamboat cruise to Fourth Lake. 116 Steamboat Landing, Old Forge.

Norridgewock Tour Boat, Stillwater Reservoir. Cruise to isolated community of Beaver River.

Thendara Golf Club. 151 5th St., Thendara.

The Adirondack Scenic Railroad runs May thru October. 84 Ford St., Thendara.

View Arts Center. 3273 Rt. 28, Old Forge.

Town of Webb Historical Association's Goodsell Museum. 2993 Rt. 28, Old Forge.

There are three miniature golf courses, a movie theater, public swimming beach and let us not forget whitewater rafting, canoeing and kayaking in the spring, summer and fall. Sportsmen have ideal hunting for big and small game.

"Webb is the Snowmobile Capital of the East" with its famous trails that take snowmobilers through the majestic woodlands of the Adirondack Mountains, and with hundreds of miles of groomed trails and snow from early December through March. It just doesn't get any better.

28

DATE: _____ WEATHER: _____

MEMORIES: _____

_____

_____

_____

_____

_____

_____

_____

_____

_____

[Passport Stamp / Signature Here]

Bald Mtn. fire tower. Restored in 1917, 35' steel tower with new interpretative signage. From Old Forge drive N on Rt. 28 4.5 miles, turn left on to Rondaxe Road and continue a quarter of a mile to the parking lot and trailhead.

Shopping:
Many quaint and unique shops can be found throughout the villages.

Old Forge Hardware has almost everything plus a huge book selection, too. 104 Fulton St.

Food & Lodging:
We have some of the best restaurants in the Adirondacks that offer all types of cuisine. Hotels, inns, B&Bs, cabins, and private house rentals are just some of the types of lodging you will find in the Town of Webb.

For more, visit www.oldforgeny.com.

Material courtesy of the Goodsell Museum, home of the Town of Webb Historical Association

A view of Fourth Lake from the restored 1917 fire tower on Bald Mountain. It's just a short hike but what an awesome view! Webb Historical Society

29

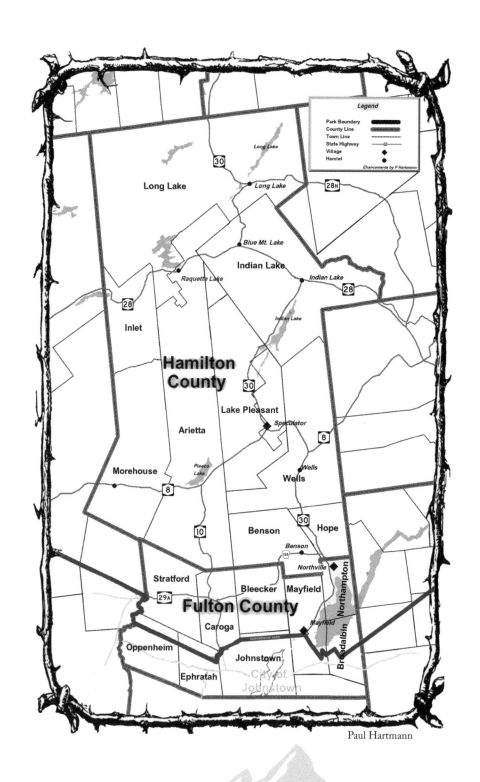

Paul Hartmann

CHAPTER 2

REGION II :

FULTON & HAMILTON COUNTIES

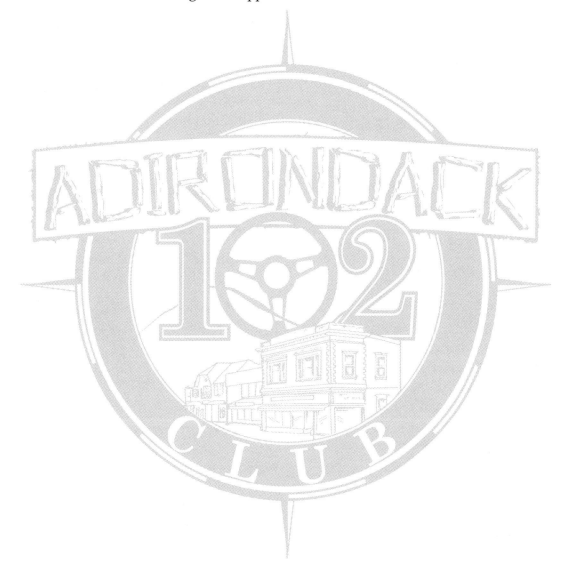

ARIETTA

The Town of Arietta in SW Hamilton County is located within the southern Adirondack Park. It includes these hamlets: Arietta, Avery's Place, Piseco, Higgins Bay, and Rudeston. Piseco Lake is approx. 7 miles long and known for its abundance of lake trout and whitefish. The word Piseco is derived from an ancient Native American word, "pisco," meaning "fish."

HISTORY

In 1836, the NYS Legislature created the town of Arietta from the Town of Lake Pleasant. By 1839 land developer Andrew K. Morehouse founded Piseco Village and established land contracts with many new settlers. Arietta was populated by woodsmen, farmers, and lumbermen. Throughout the 1800s lumber and tanning industries flourished. Prior to the turn of the 20th Century, the area became a summer tourism destination. Today, the area attracts tourists year-round with hunting, fishing, boating, hiking, snowmobiling, and camping.

POINTS OF INTEREST

Piseco Lake Historical Society & Riley Tavern Museum. Located on Old Piseco Rd. Open July and August, Saturdays and Sundays, 1 pm – 4 pm. The Riley Tavern, dating to the 1880s, is the only known Adirondack saloon to still exist in its original state. The Riley House Museum is one of the oldest buildings still standing in Arietta and contains displays relating to the town's history. Visit our page on Facebook for information and upcoming presentations.

Irondequoit Inn. A rustic retreat overlooking Piseco Lake. Established in 1892, this 600-acre retreat is a sanctuary for vacationers who value peace and quiet. 471 Old Piseco Rd., Piseco.

518-548-5500, www.irondequoitinn.com

Campgrounds:
Point Comfort, Poplar Point, and Little Sand Point are the three state campgrounds on Piseco Lake. They offer fine fishing, canoeing, sailing, and all water sports opportunities. 518-863-4545, www.dec.ny.gov.

Recreational Activities:
Hiking/Mountain Climbing on Panther Mountain Trail, T-Lake Trail, Northville-Placid Trail, and Foxey Brown Loop. Located near the hamlet of Arietta are the trails to Good Luck Lake, Jockeybush Lake, and the site of a 1933 Civilian Conservation Corps camp at Shaker Place on Rt. 10. Also, snowmobiling, skiing, snowshoeing, and ice fishing are popular.

Services:
Casey's Corner General Store. Groceries, sandwiches, lunch, deli, hot coffee, gas, liquor store, beer, and local gossip. Rt. 8, Oxbow Lake, Piseco. 518-548-3556

Piseco Airport. Municipal airport established in 1927. Old Piseco Rd. 518-548-3415

Piseco Performance Snowmobile Repair. 1610 Rt. 8, Piseco. 518-548-6000

Oxbow Lake Motel. Rt. 8, Piseco. www.oxbowlakemotel.com

Books:
Piseco Lake and Arietta by Frederick and Cynthia Adcock and *Foxey Brown* by Charles Yaple.

For more, visit www.townofarietta.com.

Material courtesy of Frederick & Cynthia Adcock, authors of *Piseco Lake and Arietta*

DATE: _____ WEATHER: _____

MEMORIES: _____

_____

_____

_____

_____

_____

_____

_____

_____

_____

_____

_____

_____

_____

_____

_____

[Passport Stamp / Signature Here]

The Irondequoit Inn is a rustic retreat overlooking Piseco Lake. Frederick & Cynthia Adcock

BENSON

Benson is the hidden gem of the Adirondacks. With 83 square miles of forested foothills threaded by dark rushing streams that gather in hollows to form still lakes before passing on beneath the eve of the pinewood, Benson is one of the last places in the mountains where travelers may truly worship in the vast tenantless silence of nature's cathedral.

Bounded by the towns of Arietta to the west, Wells to the North, Hope to the east and Bleecker and Mayfield to the south, its main thoroughfare is Co. Rt. 6, better known as the Benson Road, which departs from Rt. 30 just above the juncture where the West Stony Creek once delivered logs from the heart of timber country to the Sacandaga River, then winds westward through the hills to terminate at the Bleecker-Benson line.

Settled on lands originally claimed by the Haudenosaunee (Iroquois), Benson emerged from the wellspring of the Stony. Bringing the only skills they knew, the white settlers turned their hands toward clearing and tilling the land, logging as they pressed deep into the backwoods, sawmills lining the waterways, farms skirting the major roads as the forest fell to the axe. By mid-century, the Benson area boasted some 380 people, but by 1880 the population began to dwindle and never recovered.

Today, the town's primary claim to fame is Lapland Lake Nordic Vacation Center, located in Upper Benson off Shorer Road. Founded in 1978 by former U.S. Olympic cross-country skier Olavi Hirvonen, the Center boasts thirty miles of private trails offering excellent conditions for cross-country skiing, snowshoeing, tubing and ice skating, even in mild winters when points farther south lay

barren. Lodging is available in the Center's tupas (cabins) year-round, offering hiking, mountain biking, fishing, swimming, and (non-motorized) boating in the spring, summer and autumn months. Benson's only restaurant is located at the Center. Further accommodation may be found in seasonal camps along River Road and Townbarn Road, giving spectacular views of the Sacandaga, and only a short drive to neighboring Northville for provisions and entertainment.

Due to its preponderance of State Forest Preserve, Benson offers backwoods treasures for the casual ambler and committed bushwhacker alike, particularly along the 133-mile, 90 year-old Northville-Lake Placid Trail. Historically, the Benson portion of the trail (traditionally traversed south to north) began at a trailhead at the end of Godfrey Road in Upper Benson, crossing a right-of-way over private land before heading toward Silver Lake, some seven miles on. As this book goes to press, the trail is being rerouted, with a new southern terminus in Northville's Waterfront Park, whence hikers will pass through the village before crossing Rt. 30 and entering the woods along Gifford's Valley, winding westward through Shaker Mountain Wild Forest before swinging northbound for Benson and the Silver Lake Wilderness. The trail will emerge again on the Benson Road opposite the Woods Lake carry–an excellent short hike to the lake's sparkling southern shore–which will eventually be incorporated into the larger N-LP Trail itself. With the rerouted trail scheduled to open fully in 2016 and construction still underway, please check with the NYSDEC for completed trail sections and signposts before setting out.

For the more experienced hiker, Benson gives

DATE: _____ WEATHER: _____

MEMORIES: _____

_____

_____

_____

_____

_____

_____

_____

_____

_____

_____ [Passport Stamp / Signature Here]

access to bushwhacks across trackless State land, often along long-abandoned logging roads leading to the town's more secluded secrets, including The Notch, Three Ponds Mountain, Helldevil Dam, Ninemile Creek, Grant Lake, Cathead and Little Cathead Mountains, Kings Vly, Southerland Mountain, and Abner Creek. Benson offers excellent fishing for brook trout at Canary Pond, Grant Lake, Rock Lake and Silver Lake, as well as hunting, with white-tail deer and wild turkey particularly favored by experienced Nimrods. The stalwart photographer will find one of the most stunning views in the southern Adirondacks atop the fire tower on Cathead Mountain, now accessible only by a lengthy and difficult bushwhack since the closure of the main trail–see regional hiking guides for information.

Benson is a seductive destination for explorers seeking solitude beyond the busy byways of the Park's more frequented tourist towns.

Material courtesy of Eliza Darling, Town of Benson Resident

Two skiers relax by Lapland Lake after a busy day of cross-country skiing at the Lapland Lake Nordic Center. It was founded in 1978 by former U.S. Olympic cross-country skier, Olavi Hirvonen. The Center boasts 30 miles of private trails offering excellent conditions for cross-country skiing, snowshoeing, tubing, and ice skating. Lapland Lake Nordic Center

35

BLEECKER

The Town of Bleecker is approx. three miles north of Gloversville in Fulton Co. Its name is from Barent Bleecker, one of the original landowners of the area. It is composed of the following hamlets and lakes: Bleecker, Bleecker Center, Lindsley Corners, Peters Corners, and Chase and Mountain lakes.

HISTORY

It was established in 1831 from the Town of Johnstown. The area was sparsely settled in the late 1790s and early 1800s. Logging and lumbering and tanneries were the main businesses.

During the height of the tannery business, the town had three tanneries which led to an all-time high population of over 1000 persons in town. Ruins of one of the tanneries are still visible from the roadside via Tannery Rd. (off Barlow Rd.). Please note that the ruins are on private property.

Bleecker is one of three southern-most towns completely encompassed by the Adirondack Park. An interesting geological fact is that waters originating in the western and southern areas of town drain into the Mohawk River, while those arising in the northern and eastern portion drain into the Hudson River.

POINTS OF INTEREST

In 1858, the first (rural) Catholic Church in Fulton County was erected on a hilltop in Bleecker and could be seen for miles around. A shrine marking the site can be seen on Shrine Rd., off the Persch Rd. Of three other churches active in the late 1800s, only the original St. John's Lutheran Church on Co. Rt. 112 (now the Bleecker Community Church) is still

standing. The balcony of this church exhibits some original wood grain work.

An 1870s one-room school is maintained by a private family as the "Old School Museum," located off the Lily Lake Rd. Inquire locally or visit www.theoldschoolmuseum.org.

Explore the ruins of a late 1800s tannery. Go to Co. Rt. 145 and take the Barlow Rd. to the Tannery Rd. The ruins are on the south side of the road.

Activities:
Fishing and boating on local lakes and hiking on state property are popular in the summer. Winter affords skiing, snowshoeing, and snowmobiling on the Fulton County trail system.

Today the town is largely a bedroom community with residents commuting to employment outside the town. Visitors will find no overnight accommodations in town and should make arrangements in nearby Gloversville or Johnstown if they wish to explore the area of the southern Adirondacks for a few days.

Currently there is one local café open six days a week in town.

To inquire locally with the Town Clerk for contacts and directions, call 518-725-8382.

Material courtesy of Eleanor Brooks, Town of Bleecker Historian

DATE: _____   WEATHER: _____

MEMORIES: _____

_____

_____

_____

_____

_____

_____

_____

_____

_____

_____

_____

_____

_____

_____

[Passport Stamp / Signature Here]

The Old School Museum on Lily Lake Rd. in Bleecker. Eleanor Brooks

BROADALBIN

Broadalbin is one of the first towns organized in present-day Fulton County. It is located in the east central part of the county. The town includes the Village of Broadalbin and the hamlets of Benedict, North Broadalbin, Union Mills, and Stevers Mills. In the fall various activities take place at the Eagle Mills Cider Company location.

The name Broadalbin was given by the early Scottish settlers who came from the Breadalbane area of Scotland.

The first town meeting to be recognized by the State of New York was held on April 1, 1794. Broadalbin originally embraced the Town of Northampton and the northern portion of the Town of Perth.

The Kennyetto is the largest creek flowing through our town. The name Kennyetto is an Indian name, meaning "Snake trying to swallow its tail."

In the earlier part of the nineteenth Century our town had a knitting mill, several glove shops, and many farms. Today those are a memory. Our main employer now is the Broadalbin-Perth School District.

In 1930 a significant part of our town was flooded to form the Sacandaga Reservoir. In the 1960s the name was changed to The Great Sacandaga Lake. A boat launch is located on Lakeview Road where the public can launch their water craft and park their vehicles. This body of water is popular for boating, canoeing, and fishing in the warm months and also draws crowds in the winter for ice fishing contests and snowmobiling.

A well-known Broadalbin resident in days gone by was Robert W. Chambers who wrote over 100 books and novels. The location of his former mansion is on North Street in the Village of Broadalbin.

On the shores of the Great Sacandaga Lake is the Sacandaga Bible Conference, in operation since 1936 and growing steadily. It offers many types of religious programs throughout the year. The camp is located on the southern end of Lakeview Rd., which connects with Fulton Co. Rt. 110. You may contact the Bible Conference as well as read about their opportunities by going to Sacandagabibleconference.com.

For additional information, visit the Fulton County Visitors Center located at the intersection of Rt. 29 and Rt. 30 in Vail Mills. You may reach them online at Fulton County Visitor Center, Fulton County NY. www.fultoncountyny.gov

Material courtesy of Gordon Cornell, Town of Broadalbin Historian

DATE: _____ WEATHER: _____

MEMORIES: _____
_____
_____
_____
_____
_____
_____
_____
_____
_____
_____
_____
_____
_____
_____
_____

[Passport Stamp / Signature Here]

Broadalbin Knitting Co., Broadalbin, N. Y.

The Broadalbin Knitting Co. was in production in the early part of the 19th Century.
Gordon Cornell

CAROGA

The Town of Caroga, derived from a Native American word for "on the side of a creek," was formed in the southern tier of the Adirondack Mountains in 1842. The 30,000-acre tract includes 836 year-round residents according to the 2010 census although that number quadruples with summer residents. The town forms part of the northern boundary of Fulton County, established in 1838.

Prominent lakes include East and West Caroga Lake, Canada Lake, West Lake, Green Lake, Pine Lake, East Stoner Lake and West Stoner Lake as well as Nine Corners Lake which can only be reached by a hiking path. The main features of the town are forest, hills, mountains, creeks, and lakes as well as several smaller ponds. There is little land worth cultivating.

A statue of Nick Stoner looks out over the municipal golf course bearing his name as a frontier hero of both the Revolutionary War and War of 1812 who made the area his home. As a friend of James Fenimore Cooper, Stoner is thought to be the origin of the Natty Bumpo character in the Leatherstocking Tales.

This four-season recreation area features hiking, swimming, fishing, hunting, skiing, rock climbing, kayaking, camping, snowmobiling, golfing, ice car racing, sailing, cross-country skiing, snowshoeing, and off-road hill climbs.

POINTS OF INTEREST

Starting at the southern border as Rt. 10 enters the town, Royal Mountain Ski Area boasts winter alpine skiing and summer hill climbs. On Rt. 29A a state-sponsored campsite and beach rests on East Caroga Lake. Caroga Lake State Park has 161 campsites and has swimming fishing and boating. For more, visit www.dec.ny.gov/outdoor/24458.html.

Continuing north on Rt. 29A one passes several restaurants, historic Sherman's Amusement Park, and Vrooman's Hotel. Taking the "Y" on the left will bring you to the Caroga Museum within 100 yards while proceeding north on combined Rt. 29A/10 to the right will bring you to the town hall, municipal picnic area, and golf course. Another mile will bring you to Canada Lake Marina and Store where you can get groceries, gifts, sandwiches, books, and all your boating needs (www.canadalakemarine.com). Three more miles will bring you to Pine Lake Park public beach and camp grounds. It has 75 campsites and cabin rentals, located at 136 Timberline Lane, Caroga Lake.

A hiking trail from Green Lake Road, across from the marina, leads up Kane Mountain to a historic fire tower where views of the surrounding mountains and lakes are picture perfect.

At the next intersection, Rt. 29A leads westward within 100 yards to the Nine Corners Lake hiking trail where a 20-minute hike brings you to a beautiful vista, fishing, and hiking as well as a boulder field that has become a favorite with rock climbers. Taking the "Y" to the north leads to East and West Stoner Lakes.

There is a coffee shop at the intersection of Rts. 112 & 309, Caroga Lake.

Find lodging on Caroga Lake; at Vrooman's Hotel, located at the intersection of Rts. 10 & 29A, and at Nick Stooner Inn, located at 1810 Rt. 10.

DATE: _____ WEATHER: _____

MEMORIES: _____

_____

_____

_____

_____

_____

_____

_____

_____

_____

_____

_____

_____

_____

[Passport Stamp / Signature Here]

For more information, go to:

www.carogatimes.com
www.carogalake.com
www.royalmountain.com
www.dec.ny.gov/outdoor/24458.html
www.pinelakepark.com/site/home.html

Material courtesy of Richard Nilsen,
Town of Caroga Historian

There are three trails to the restored Kane Mountain fire
tower but most hikers take the easiest trail near Green Lake.
It can be reached by going 3 miles north of the junction of
Rts. 10 and 29A in the Village of Caroga Lake. Turn right
onto Green Lake Road and drive along the lake. Take the fork
to the left at the end of the lake. There is a parking area at the
trailhead. Follow the trail markers 0.9 mile to the tower. This
is a short easy hike for the whole family. Paul Hartmann

41

EPHRATAH

The Town of Ephratah was created by dividing the Town of Palatine in two parts. The northern section became known as The Town of Ephratah, named by Anthony Beck. The name comes from the Bible and means "abundance-bearing fruit."

Ephratah's landscape is very hilly with elevations from 400 to 1,500 feet above the Mohawk River. The town is bounded on the north by the Town of Stratford, on the east by the Town of Johnstown, and on the west by the Town of Oppenheim.

Within the Town of Ephratah there are four hamlets: Garoga, Rockwood, Lassellsville, and Ephratah. Garoga, Rockwood, and Ephratah are located on the Caroga Creek and used the water to power various mills. Lassellsville, located on the Zimmerman Creek, was surrounded by forest and there were many sawmills built on the creek

PLACES OF INTEREST

Saltsmans Hotel, which was built in 1832, is in the hamlet of Ephratah on Rt. 10. It has an old-fashioned decor and serves dinners, Thursday thru Sunday, from Easter to Halloween. People come from all around for very tasty meals.

Royal Mountain Campsites is a nightly stop-in but many people come and stay for the summer. Granny's Ice Cream at the campsite is a very busy place on warm summer nights and is open from 11 am – 10 pm, from the middle of April to Columbus Day. It is located at the intersection of Rt. 29 & Rt.10, west of Rockwood.

Brittany's Diner. 105 St. Hwy 67, Ephratah.

Top of The Hill Grill. 4700 Rt. 29, Johnstown.

The Ephratah Recreation Commission located on Rt. 29 (2 miles west of Granny's) is a good way for children to get outside and play softball and soccer. A walking path circles the athletic fields for everyone to use.

Rockwood Dam located on Rt. 10 on the north edge of Rockwood is a good place to go kayaking, canoeing, or fishing.

Frasiers Sugar Shack (144 Church St., 2 miles north of Lassellsville. Take Rt. 29 to Co. Rt. 119 to Church St.) and The Mud Road Sugar House (278 Mud Rd.) both participate in the NYS Maple Syrup Producers Association. Open houses are held during the last two weekends in March.

Some of the town roads are connecters to the major snowmobile trails in Fulton County as found on the Fulton County Highway and Snowmobile map.

Material courtesy of Evelyn Frasier, Town of Ephratah Historian

DATE: _____ WEATHER: _____

MEMORIES: _____

_____

_____

_____

_____

_____

_____

_____

_____

_____

_____

_____

_____

_____

_____

_____

[Passport Stamp / Signature Here]

People come from all around to enjoy the very tasty meals at the 1832 Saltsmans Hotel on Rt. 10 in the hamlet of Ephratah. Jason Hainsworth

43

HOPE

The Town of Hope is located in southern Hamilton County within the boundaries of the Adirondack Park. The town population is 392. It is largely forested with the vast majority being state land. The lands were originally owned by the Turtle Clan of the Mohawk Indians. On July 31, 1772 Chief Hendricks signed Bergens Purchase of 19,589 acres by drawing a turtle as a signature.

HISTORY

The Town of Hope was formed in 1818. By 1825 there were over 2,000 acres cleared for farming. Sawmills, farming, and tanneries were the mainstay. By 1850 the population was 1,125.

In the late 1800s inns and hotels flourished. By the early 1900s, the population dwindled to 163 with development to the north of Hope and tanneries moving south to Gloversville. The sound of sawmills and double-edged axes was no more. The cleared land was reclaimed by nature. Tourism continued with hotels, inns, and taverns. The Rt.30 corridor provided gas stations, tourist cabins, lodging, and restaurants.

Eventually Hope evolved into a mountainous residential community, much as it is today. Largely undeveloped with glistening lakes and streams, rolling hills, and peaceful valleys, it is appealing to sportsmen, hunters, fishermen, hikers, and outdoor enthusiasts.

RECREATION

The Sacandaga River flows adjacent to Rt. 30. Popular activities include canoeing, kayaking, fishing, and tubing. Park at the Town Hall and float downstream to the Great Sacandaga Lake.

Groffs Creek has a hiking path that passes three waterfalls. It is located at the end of River Rd. on the west side of the Sacandaga River.

There are three lakes accessible from the trailhead on Creek Rd. in Hope Falls: Bennett Lake, Middle Lake, and Murphy Lake.

The East Stoney Creek flows through the Hope Valley. Follow Hope Falls Rd. to the end of the pavement and continue on the dirt road located on state lands. There are designated camping sites adjacent to the creek. At the end of the road there is a trailhead for Wilcox Lake and Tenant Creek's three falls.

Hope is a tranquil, friendly place; a proud and cordial community of good neighbors.

Material courtesy of Roy Edwardsen, Town of Hope Historian

DATE: _____ WEATHER: _____

MEMORIES: _____

_____

_____

_____

_____

_____

_____

_____

_____

_____

_____

_____

_____

_____

_____

_____

[Passport Stamp / Signature Here]

East Stoney Creek from Creek Rd. Bridge in Hope. Roy Edwardsen

45

INDIAN LAKE

Indian Lake is located in the central Adirondacks, at the intersection of Rts. 28 & 30 in Hamilton, Co. It includes Indian Lake, Blue Mountain Lake, and Sabael.

HISTORY

Indian Lake was established in 1858 from the towns of Gilman, Long Lake, and Wells. In 1861, Indian Lake was expanded using territory from Gilman and Lake Pleasant. In the mid-1800s Indian Lake's wealth of lakes and rivers was the 'highway' that enabled the logging industry to meet the needs of a growing nation. Today those same resources are used by tourists and second home owners for rafting kayaking, and hiking in the reforested woods.

INTERESTING PLACES TO VISIT

Adirondack Lakes Center for the Arts provides cultural events during the summer. Rt. 28, Blue Mt. Lake. 877-752-7715, www.adirondackarts.org

The Indian Lake Theater located on Main St. Indian Lake it is a non-profit multi-purpose community center, a space for the same great movies that have been showing for years, plus community theater, concerts and special events. 518-648-5950, www.indianlaketheater.org

Long Lake Library is located on Pelon Road. 518-648-5444

Abanakee Studios has antiques, gifts, books, gallery, and workshops. Rt. 28 and LaVergne Rd., Indian Lake.

Timberlock Camp, est. 1899, is a family resort with 23 cabins on Indian Lake. Open air dining hall overlooks Indian Lake with 3 home-cooked meals provided daily. Facilities include children's beach, water skiing, tennis, sailing, hiking, horseback riding, biking, & archery range. 160 Farrington Way, Rt. 30 Sabael. www.timberlock.com

Outdoor Recreation:
Cedar River Golf Club. 9-hole course, driving range, restaurant & motel. 180 West Main St., Indian Lake. www.cedarrivergolf.com

Adventure Sports Rafting Co. 6127 Rt. 28, Indian Lake. www.adventuresportsrafting.com

Adventure Rafting Co. 100 E Main St., Indian Lake. 518-523-1635

Blue Mountain Fire Tower, a two-mile trail leads to a fire tower with views of the central Adirondacks. The trailhead is located on Rt. 30 just above the Adirondack Museum in Blue Mt. Lake.

Historic Three Lake Tour offers a two-hour scenic boat cruise in one of our original 1916 wooden launches. Blue Mt. Lake Boat Livery offers many kinds of boat rentals. www.boatlivery.com/tours.html

Camping:
Lake Durant State Campground is located on the east shore of 327-acre Lake Durant. 3444 Rt. 30, Blue Mt. Lake.

DEC State Indian Lake Islands Campground is 12 miles north of Speculator on Rt. 30 in Sabael.

Historic Locations:
Adirondack Museum: Its vast campus features displays in 22 modern exhibition galleries and historic buildings. The exhibitions tell the story of the Adirondacks and its people. There are plenty of indoor and outdoor activities for kids, too. It also has a large gift/book store. Open

DATE: _____ WEATHER: _____

MEMORIES: _____

_____

_____

_____

_____

_____

_____

_____

_____

_____

_____

_____

_____

_____

_____

[Passport Stamp / Signature Here]

May thru October, 10 am – 5 pm.
9097 Rt. 30, Blue Mt. Lake.
www.adkmuseum.org

Indian Lake Museum is located at
Rts. 28/30, Indian Lake, contains
displays relating to the historic
Indian population. Open June thru
October, Thursday - Sunday,
1 pm – 3 pm.

Material courtesy of William
R. Zullo, Town of Indian Lake
Historian

The entrance to the Adirondack Museum in Blue Mtn. Paige Doerner

INLET

Nestled 1,818 feet above sea level, at the head of Fourth Lake and along the shore of the channel into tiny Fifth Lake, lies the community of Inlet on Rt. 28 in western Hamilton County. Often called the "Mountain Village of Beautiful Lakes," it is surrounded by mountains and looks down the expanse of Fourth Lake to spectacular sunsets at the western end.

Formerly part of the Town of Moorehouse, the area was separated and established as the Town of Inlet in January 1902. Originally home to many hotels, the guests were transported by large and picturesque steamboats as roads were few. Hockey was a favorite sport in the early days, with teams coming from as far as Canada to participate. Probably the most spectacular feature of the town was the 660-foot toboggan run built in 1935. It hurled courageous souls from high over the road out onto the frozen Fourth Lake, ending in a slide far across the lake. This was removed in 1942.

Today, snowmobile and cross-country ski trails invite tourists for winter sports. Rocky Mountain is an easy climb and offers an outstanding view of the village and the lakes below. It is south of Inlet on Rt. 28 and the trailhead parking is on the right. At this parking area is the trailhead to Black Bear Mountain Trail that is also popular with tourists.

A well-equipped Clark's Marina on Rt. 28 offers access to boating needs.

The Inlet Golf Club at 300 Rt. 28 has recently expanded to 18 holes and has a renovated clubhouse. The town also has a public beach and public tennis courts.

The main street in the village boasts of a lovely library, gift shops, and a new Historical Building. Also of historical interest is the Inlet Common School at 220 Rt. 28. Though not quite a one-room school, each teacher has two classes from kindergarten through sixth grade housed in two small buildings overlooking Fifth Lake.

The Adirondack Reader bookstore is at 156 Main Street. It has a wide selection including Adirondack books, gifts, maps, and postcards.

The Woods Inn (1894) is one of the original buildings at 148 Main St. and Rt. 28 in Inlet. There is a tavern, dining room, great room, and lake-side cottages. It has been restored and welcomes guests. www.thewoodsinn.com

There are also several lovely public campsites on some of the smaller lakes in the area, as well as several housekeeping units and a motel.

Inlet retains the charm of a small Adirondack community while having many attractions for tourists.

For more information, visit www.inletny.com.

Material courtesy of Letty Haynes,
Town of Inlet Historian & Mitch Lee,
Resident and Writer

DATE: _____ WEATHER: _____

MEMORIES: _____

_____

_____

_____

_____

_____

_____

_____

_____

_____

_____

_____

_____

_____

[Passport Stamp / Signature Here]

Arrowhead Park is located in downtown Inlet and offers swimming, tennis, a playground, a picnic area, and concerts. www.inletny.com

JOHNSTOWN

The Town of Johnstown is located in Fulton County in the foothills of the Adirondacks. It begins just north of the Mohawk River and extends to inside the Blue Line of the Adirondack Park. The town includes two cities, Johnstown and Gloversville, and the hamlets of Dennies Crossing, Hale Mills, Kecks Center, Meco, Pleasant Square, Progress, Samsonsville, and West Bush.

Johnstown was founded by Sir William Johnson in 1762. Johnson received a patent from King George for his service during the French and Indian War. It was here that he built himself a plantation and manor house. The village that he created to support it was named for his son John, hence the original name "John's Town."

Johnson's home has been restored by New York State and is open for tours. In addition to his home, there are a number of other structures that date from the time.

The Fulton County Courthouse was built by Johnson in 1772 and still in use today as the oldest continuously used courthouse in the United States. The Historical Society has a museum and maintains the "Drumm House" which depicts colonial life during Johnson's time. In addition the Historical Society conducts tours of the Colonial Cemetery on Tuesday evenings during the summer.

Originally the seat of Montgomery County, Johnstown was formed in 1793. In 1808 the core of the town was incorporated as a village.

Johnstown is also the site of what was the last battle of the American Revolution. The battle of Johnstown was fought behind Johnson Hall on October 25, 1781, just six days after the surrender at Yorktown.

Another famous citizen is Elizabeth Cady-Stanton the organizer of the Seneca Falls Convention and founder of the Women's Suffrage movement. She was born in Johnstown in 1815 the daughter of Judge Daniel Cady. The Historical Society Museum has a room dedicated to her along with a number of objects belonging to her and her father.

During the latter part of the 19th and for most of the 20th Centuries, Johnstown and Gloversville were the home to the leather business in the United States. There are still factory outlet stores providing leather goods in the area.

For the outdoor enthusiast, there is Peck's Lake Resort with great fishing, boat rentals, campsites, and cottages. 180 Peck's Lake Rd., Gloversville. www.peckslake.com

Johnson Hall State Historic Site. nysparks.com/historic-sites/10/details.aspx

Johnstown Community Information. www.cityofjohnstown.ny.gov

Fulton Co. Historical Society Museum. 237 Kingsboro Ave., Gloversville.

Peck's Park Schoolhouse and Museum. www.mohawkvalleymuseums.com

Daniel Storto, famous glovemaker in Gloversville. www.danielstorto.com

Swany Gloves, Gloversville Industrial Park. www.swanygloves.com

Material courtesy of Lansing Lord, Johnstown Resident & Former Historian

DATE: _____ WEATHER: _____

MEMORIES: _____

_____

_____

_____

_____

_____

_____

_____

_____

_____

_____

_____

_____

_____

_____

[Passport Stamp / Signature Here]

The Fulton County Courthouse was built by Johnson in 1772. Lansing Lord

LAKE PLEASANT & SPECULATOR

The Town of Lake Pleasant is in the southern part of Hamilton County in the southern Adirondack Mountains. It consists of the Village of Speculator, the hamlet of Lake Pleasant, and 12 lakes: Buckhorn, Fawn, Gilman, Hamilton, Lake Pleasant, Lewey, Mud, Oxbow, Sacandaga, Vly, Whitaker, and the southern part of Indian Lake.

History

Settlers came to the area about 1797 and by 1812 the Town of Lake Pleasant was established. At the western part of town the community of Lake Pleasant was formed and at the outlet of the lake was Newton's Corner, which changed its name to Speculator in 1897. The Village of Speculator was incorporated in 1925.Sportsman came to hunt, fish, and rough it in the invigorating mountain air.

By the 1850s the logging crews moved in and purchased abandoned and unsold parcels of land. Logs were floated down the Sacandaga River to the mills in Glens Falls.

By the 1880s several large hotels had been built to accommodate the increasing number of summer guests. Many of these guests soon purchased land along the lake shore and built summer cottages.

In 1914 Camp of the Woods, a Christian family camp, was started and has grown to accommodate thousands. www.camp-of-the-woods.org

Deerfoot Lodge (1929), a Christian camp for boys on Whitaker Lake, is also still going strong. Camp Fowler is a family camp still operating on Lake Sacandaga.

For winter sports there are ski slopes and trails, a toboggan run, skating rink, and hockey team.

In 1926 the Osborne Inn complex became the training ground for champion prizefighters who later became world champions: Gene Tunney, Max Baer, and Max Schmeling.

Tamarack Playhouse in Lake Pleasant had several actors who became famous: Kirk Douglas, Carl Malden, and Carl Betz.

In 1934 a Civilian Conservation Corps camp did a lot of work at Moffit Beach, Lewey Lake and Sacandaga State Parks.

Recreation:
Swimming, boating, fishing, hunting, skiing, snowmobiling, camping, and also shopping, dining and lodging.

Oak Mt. Ski area has snow-tubing and skiing. The area also has cross-country ski trails, mountain bike trails, snowmobile trails, etc. 518-548-3606, www.oakmountainski.com

The Sacandaga Pathway is a wheelchair accessible nature trail along the river with informative signs and historical photos. It is in Speculator and starts by the ball field and pavilion.

Our beautiful beach is open to the public and has lifeguards. We have a public park on Osborne's Point next to the beach. Across the road from the beach is the ballfield, pavilion, playground, basketball court, Bocci-ball court, and horeshoes.

Tennis courts are on Elm Lake Road and by the courthouse in Lake Pleasant. The Lake Pleasant Golf Course is open to the public at 2537 Rt. 8.

DATE: _____ WEATHER: _____

MEMORIES: _____

_____

_____

_____

_____

_____

_____

_____

_____

_____

_____

_____ [Passport Stamp / Signature Here]

Our annual 4th of July celebration has a parade, carnival, and fireworks on the first Saturday in July. Throughout the summer and fall there are many events held at the ballfield: an art show, craft fair, flea and farmer's markets, war re-enactments, BBQ's, concerts, an applefest, and more.

Historical Museum on Rt. 8 is open during the summer and fall by the Lake Pleasant-Speculator Historical Society. 518-548-4478

The Chamber of Commerce is at the intersection of Rts. 8 & 30. www.speculatorchamber.com

Material courtesy of Beverly Hoffman, Town of Speculator Historian

An old postcard depicting the Osborne Inn on Lake Pleasant. Beverly & Shorty Hoffman

53

LONG LAKE

The Town of Long Lake was settled in the 1830s and is the most northern town in Hamilton County. It is the second largest town in land area in New York including 449 square miles encompassing the Whitney Wilderness, Brandreth Park, Raquette Lake, and the 14-mile Long Lake. In 1869 William H. H. Murray wrote the bestseller, *Adventures in the Wilderness,* which opened up the tourism industry in Raquette Lake and Long Lake. Hotels large and small opened for business.

Getting to Raquette and Long Lake was difficult in the mid-19th Century. The trip to Long Lake was accomplished by night boat from NYC to Albany, train to North Creek, stagecoach to Blue Mountain Lake and guideboat via the Raquette River to Long Lake. By the late 1800s the Lake Champlain-Carthage Road and William Seward Webb's Mohawk and Malone Railway were built making travel to the area more convenient.

Raquette Lake initially was served by train from Utica and by boat through the Fulton Chain and Carries to the lake. By the late 1890s the train came all the way to Raquette Lake. Passengers to Blue Mountain Lake were served by steamboat from Raquette Lake to the Marion River Carry RR, the smallest standard gauge RR in the world, to Utowana Lake where a steamboat carried them to their destinations on Blue Mountain Lake.

Camps were built by William West Durant for notables J.P. Morgan, the Vanderbilt family, the Huntingtons, and members of the Carnegie family in Raquette Lake. The Rev. Joseph Duryea, Henry S. Harper and politicians such as Judge Green of NYC and Senator Orville Platt from Connecticut constructed more modest camps on Long Lake.

Popular activities in and around Long Lake include fishing, paddling, hiking, snowmobiling, and relaxing.

INTERESTING PLACES TO VISIT

Buttermilk Falls. Northpoint Rd., Long Lake.

Great Camp Sagamore. Great Camp Sagamore dates from 1897 and was the wilderness retreat of the Alfred G. Vanderbilt family from 1901-1954. A 27-building complex, it is now a National Historic Landmark. Sagamore Rd., Raquette Lake. www.greatcampsagamore.org

Hoss's Country Corner. A landmark in the central Adirondacks that has groceries, gifts, souvenirs, and Adirondack books. Don't miss their Author Night on the second Tuesday in August at 7 pm.

Helms Aero Service. 1250 Main St., Long Lake, 15 minute flights with spectacular aerial views of the Adirondacks. 518-624-3931

Raquette Lake Navigation offers dining cruises and sightseeing. 315-354-5532, www.rlnavigation.com

Adirondack Hotel. Operating since the mid-1800s. Past guests include Helen Keller, President McKinley, and Mickey Mantle. Open year-round with lodging and restaurant. 1245 Main St., Long Lake. 518-624-4700, www.adirondackhotel.com

Eagle Rock. Located at the northern end of Long Lake, nine miles north of the village, only accessible by boat! Spectacular views of the Seward and Santanoni mountains.

Long Lake Boat Tours. 518-624-LAKE (5253), www.longlakeboattours.com

DATE: _____ WEATHER: _____

MEMORIES: _____

_____

_____

_____

_____

_____

_____

_____

_____

_____

_____

_____

_____

_____

[Passport Stamp / Signature Here]

Places to Hike:
Northville-Lake Placid Trail, located at Rt. 28 N. Follows the eastern shore of Long Lake. Discover Caitlin Bay, Kelly's Point, Rodney Point, and Plumley's Landing.

Death Brook Falls. 3.6 miles east of Raquette Lake on Rt. 28. Short path and great photo opportunity.

Owls Head Mountain. Restored fire tower and breathtaking views. Endion Rd., Long Lake.

Sargent Pond Loop. North Point Rd., Long Lake.

Mt. Sabattis Recreation & Picnic Area. Views of downtown Long Lake, accessible from the municipal park. 6 Pavilion Way, Long Lake.

Material courtesy of Alexandra Roalsvig, Long Lake Director of Tourism and Abbie Verner, Long Lake archivist

In the 1800s there was a floating bridge over the widening Raquette River to the Kellogg House in Long Lake. Today it is called the Adirondack Hotel. Alexandra Roalsvig

55

MAYFIELD

The town and village of Mayfield are located in the eastern section of Fulton County in the southern Adirondacks. Its main road is Rt. 30. The southwestern shore of the Great Sacandaga Lake is in the Town of Mayfield.

Mayfield is part of the Sacandaga Valley, which was once in an ancient ocean as seen by the many fossils found in the sedimentary rock. It was then covered by a glacier which left the large rocks we see in the soil and shoreline when it receded.

Sacandaga is a Mohawk word meaning 'the land of waving grass'. There were four large creeks that flowed through Mayfield filling its valley to create the Vlaie ('swampy area'). Before being flooded the Vlaie was considered to have the best fishing and hunting in the state.

The Town of Mayfield was one of the first three towns created in Fulton County. On March 12, 1793 it was set off from Caughnawaga (a Mohawk village from 1666 to 1693 near the village of Fonda), and was fully organized as a town on the 1st of April 1794. The town received its name from the Mayfield Patent which was granted on June 27, 1770. Sir William Johnson was responsible for the first settlement in 1760, and it was called 'Philadelphia Bush'. This took place on an Indian trail/road that led from Tribes Hill to the Sacandaga River and crossed the entire width of the town. Johnson wanted settlers in the area along the trail so that he'd have safe passage to his home at Summer House Point. Farming was the primary occupation in the earliest years. Mayfield's natural resources were lumber and limestone that was kilned and used for tanning.

Mayfield had many hamlets within its boundary: Riceville, Munsonville, Wilkins' Corners, Woodworth's Corners, Vail Mills, Jackson Summit, Shawville, Closeville, Cranberry Creek, Red Bunch, Tolman Town, and Anthonyville. Each in its time was a thriving community. The close proximity of the tanneries allowed glove manufacturing to become the main industry from the mid-1800s through the 1960s. Coleco Inc. replaced the Glove factories operating a plastic extrusion plant. Like all the towns and villages in the Sacandaga Valley, the 1930 building of the Conklinville Dam and flooding of the valley changed the fabric of Mayfield. Land, homes, and businesses were lost along with the Vlaie. The positives for Mayfield with the creation of The Great Sacandaga Lake were the recreational benefits it provides.

PLACES OF INTEREST

Mayfield Town Beach, and picnic area. Burr Road (off Rt. 30) just past Co. Rt. 123.

Wildlife Museum. A collection of over 500 hunting, fishing and trapping artifacts, arrows and arrowheads, and full-size mounts of bears, wolves, buffalo, mountain lions, fish, and birds. 3747 Rt. 30, Amsterdam.

Adirondack Animal Land. The largest zoo in Upstate NY with over 500 animals including colorful birds, camels bear, and deer. It also has a 25-acre African Safari ride with a 35-acre walk-through area. 3554 Rt. 30, Gloversville.

Rice Homestead. The two-story home was built in 1810 (the original house was built in 1790) by Oliver Rice, a Revolutionary War soldier. The Homestead is now maintained as a

DATE: _____ WEATHER: _____

MEMORIES: _____

_____

_____

_____

_____

_____

_____

_____

_____

_____

_____

[Passport Stamp / Signature Here]

museum by the Mayfield Historical Society. It contains historical treasures from the Rice family and the Mayfield area. Open Wednesday & Saturday afternoons during the summer. Directions: Going north on Rt. 30 take first left after intersection of Rt. 30A (at Mr. Softee's), then turn left at the stop sign. The Homestead is on the left. 328 Riceville Rd., Mayfield.

Riceville Cemetery is located on Co. Rt. 102 and is the resting place of over 200 former residents.

Woodworth Cemetery dates back to 1795. Located on W Main St. near Beech St.

The winter season brings ice fishing, cross-country skiing on the school's groomed trails, snowshoeing and snowmobiling on miles of trails and the Sacandaga Lake.

For area tourism, news, and events:
www.44lakes.com
www.sacandagaexpress.com
www.visitsacandaga.com
www.mayfieldny.org
www.sacandagalife.com.

Material courtesy of an Anonymous Resident of Mayfield Village & Town

The 1810 Rice Homestead is decorated for the Christmas Open House in December. Doug Sieg

57

MOREHOUSE

The Town of Morehouse is located in the southwestern corner of Hamilton County on Rt. 8, approx. 22 miles north of Little Falls, in the southwestern Adirondack Mountains. It includes the hamlets of Morehouse and Hoffmeister.

Morehouse was formed from the Town of Lake Pleasant in 1835. A portion of the town was subsequently carved off as part of the Town of Long Lake. In 1901, the Town of Inlet was formed from the northern end of the town. Morehouse now boasts the smallest population in Hamilton, but it is a hidden gem.

PLACES TO VISIT

The Methodist Church was opened in 1835 but due to low attendance and declining population, it closed its doors in 1989 as a church. Historian, Carol Ford, opened it again in 1991 as a museum thus preserving one of our historic buildings. Each year new exhibits are added. Volunteers Diane Farber and Janice Reynolds assist when the museum is open. The museum is located on Rt. 8 across from the Morehouse Fire Company. Open Labor Day thru Memorial Day, Saturdays & Sundays, 12 Noon – 3 pm.

There are three cemeteries that are town-maintained: The Methodist Cemetery on Rt. 8 behind the Methodist Church Museum; the Catholic Cemetery on Rt. 8, and the Mountain Home Cemetery on Mountain Home Rd.

RECREATION

Living or visiting in Morehouse affords everyone the luxury of a serene and peaceful community with sparkling streams and beautiful mountains. The popular West

Canada Creek and nearby lakes provide ample fishing, boating, kayaking, canoeing, and camping activities in the spring and summer. Hunting for turkey, bear or deer will keep you busy in the spring and fall months. Winter months bring a flurry of activity with vast areas which offer easy access for cross-country skiing, and snowshoeing.

Morehouse offers some of the best groomed snowmobile trails in the region. The trails take you through snow-covered scenic woodlands for a true snowmobile experience. The trails are free to all, and with two very simple requests. Please be respectful of landowners and their property. Also give our groomers the right of way so that your riding experience will be safe and enjoyable.

Annual Events:
The town of Morehouse is a quiet community, but it boasts a network of hardworking people who show pride in their community. Annual events sponsored by local clubs, the Fire Department, and the town include Feb Fest, Chinese Auction, Kid's Fishing Derby, Morehouse Day, Fall Turkey Dinner, and The Rod and Gun Club's Wild Game Dinner.

Whether you enjoy outdoor activities or prefer to sit by a cozy fire, read a good book, or simply enjoy the scenery, we think you will enjoy our town. Stop by and say hello, you might decide to stay!

For more, visit www.townofmorehouse.com.

Material courtesy of Bill Farber, Town of Morehouse Supervisor

DATE: _____ WEATHER: _____

MEMORIES: _____

_____

_____

_____

_____

_____

_____

_____

_____

_____

_____

_____

_____

_____

_____

[Passport Stamp / Signature Here]

The 1835 Methodist Church that is now a museum.
www.townofmorehouseny.com

NORTHAMPTON TOWN

The Town of Northampton is in the northeastern corner of Fulton County approx. 12 miles NE of Gloversville on Rt. 30. It consists of the village of Northville and the hamlets of Fish House, Sacandaga Park, Carpenters Corners, and Sweets Crossing.

The town was formed from part of Broadalbin in 1799. The town was named after a 6,000-acre tract of land called the Northampton Patent. At one time the Sacandaga River flowed through the town before the river was dammed up to create the Great Sacandaga Lake. Within the town were several small hamlets; Osborne Bridge, Parkville, Denton's Corner's, Fish House, and Cranberry Creek which were all either totally or partially inundated by the flooding.

POINTS OF INTEREST

Northampton State Park is one of the largest in NY State. It has 224 campsites, picnic area, boat launch, and sandy beach. Location: Take Rt. 30N and turn onto Rt. 152. Then take first right turn onto Houseman St. The park will be at the very end of that road. Open from Memorial Day weekend until mid-October. 328 Houseman St., Mayfield.

Public Boat Launch, about an eighth of a mile north of the Northville Bridge on Rt. 30.

Hamlet of Historic Fish House, located at the southern end of the town and the Great Sacandaga Lake. Sir William Johnson built a lodge he called Fish House prior to the Revolutionary War. Some of the battles took place in this hamlet. Visit the Fish House website at www.northamptonnyhistory.com.

Sacandaga Park located half a mile south of the Northville Bridge The park began as a Methodist Campground. When the FJ & G Railroad was extended to Northville, the park expanded into a picnic area, and eventually became "the Coney Island of the North," with a huge amusement park, hotels, and many private camps. The Methodists moved out when the park became too "worldly." As many as 5,000 visitors arrived by train on a weekend. When the Sacandage River was dammed up in Conklinville, the amusement park was demolished and the train tracks were removed, so the Park was drastically changed. Today it consists of a golf course, a couple of restaurants, and summer homes of which some have been winterized.

The Old Sacandaga RR Station has been refurbished and can be rented by the week. www.sacandagastation.com

Sacandaga Golf Club: This 9-hole course is located in the Sacandaga Park. The semi-private course opened originally in 1898, and was owned by the FJ & G Railroad in the 1930s. The course is one of the five oldest continually running golf courses in New York State. www.sacandagaexpress.com

Grandview Mini Golf Course overlooks the Great Sacandaga Lake. 291 Houseman St., near the Northampton Beach State Park.

Material courtesy of Gail Cramer, Town of Northampton Historian

DATE: _____ WEATHER: _____

MEMORIES: _____

_____

_____

_____

_____

_____

_____

_____

_____

_____

_____

_____

_____

_____

_____

_____

[Passport Stamp / Signature Here]

The Northville/Northampton Historical
Museum is at 421 South Main St. in
Northville. Gail Cramer

61

NORTHVILLE VILLAGE

The Village of Northville is in the northeast corner of Fulton County 33 miles north of Amsterdam on Rt. 30. Its population in 2010 was 1,099. The village is on the southwestern shores of the Great Sacandaga Lake.

The village was first settled around 1786. It was originally named Sacandaga until the postmaster, Joseph Spier, changed the name to Northville in 1827, because it was the village farthest north in Fulton Co. to have a post office. Northville was incorporated in 1873, setting itself off from the Town of Northampton.

Northville was on high ground along the Sacandaga River. Then the Sacandaga Valley was cleared of towns and farms to make a dam and reservoir to protect towns along the Hudson River against flooding. The Conklinville Dam was completed in 1929 and in 1930 the Sacandaga Valley was flooded creating the Great Sacandaga Lake that reached to the edge of the village.

INTERESTING PLACES TO VISIT

Northville/Northampton Historical Museum. Open July and August on Wednesdays and Saturdays, 10 am – 2 pm. Also open by request June through October. 421 South Main St. 518-863-2628

Bradt Museum, consisting of Paul Bradt's hunting trophies and his hunting experiences. Located in the Municipal Building at 412 South Main St. Visit when the town and village offices are open. 518-863-4040

Ira Gray Museum. A local trapper, woodsman, and author of several Adirondack books. Gray advised people who wanted a long life, "Don't smoke, don't drink and don't work inside." See his stuffed animals and wood carvings. Located in the Municipal Building located at 412 South Main Street. Open when the town and village offices are open.

Waterfront Park is new and is the gateway to the Northville-Lake Placid trail, a popular hiking trail winding through the Adirondack Mountains.

Farmers' Market is open every Friday, May 24th through October 11th, 2 pm – 5 pm. 162 South Main St.

Tuesday Farmers' Market is open rain or shine, July through Columbus Day weekend, 2 pm – 5 pm.

Town Park has picnic tables, benches, beautiful flowers and trees, and a gazebo with picnic tables. Located next to the historical museum and municipal building on South Main St.

Great Sacandaga Lake provides much entertainment, winter and summer. A great place to waterski, kayak, canoe, sail or just cruise around the lake. During the winter months there are ice fishing contests, snowmobile races, ice skating, and even motorcycle races on the lake.

Hiking:
There are many hiking trails in the area. The most famous is the Northville-Lake Placid trail that begins in the village at Waterfront Park.

Village Tours are often offered by either the NNHS or AARCH.

Material courtesy of Gail Cramer, Historian of Northville and Northampton

DATE: _____ WEATHER: _____

MEMORIES: _____

_____

_____

_____

_____

_____

_____

_____

_____

_____

_____

_____

_____

_____

_____

[Passport Stamp / Signature Here]

Bradt Museum has a collection of logging, hunting, fishing, and other
settler history. It is located on South Main St. Gail Cramer

OPPENHEIM

The Town of Oppenheim is in the western corner of Fulton County and northeast of Little Falls. Its population in 2010 was 1,924. The town consists of the eastern part of the village of Dolgeville and these hamlets: Oppenheim Center, Crum Creek, Kringsbush, Lotville, Middle Sprite, and Youker's Bush.

The first settlers of Oppenheim were Palatine Germans who came from Oppenheim, around 1791. A significant number of immigrants from the New England states, some veterans of the Continental Army who had served in the Mohwak Valley during the Revolution, settled in Oppenheim from the early 1790s. One of our local cemeteries has six Revolutionary War veterans, and we have three veterans of the Battle of Bunker Hill who came here as settlers and are buried in other family cemeteries.

The Town of Oppenheim was set off from the Town of Palatine, Montgomery County on March 18, 1808. The principal occupation in the 1800s was farming and raising stock animals. There were seven cheese factories. Oppenheim also had many sawmills. Lumbering was a principal means of making a living up into the 1890s when competition from the Northeast and the Northwest, plus the decline in available forests, put this industry into a decline.

Dolgeville, in the southern foothills of the Adirondacks, is named after Alfred Dolge (1848-1922) a world-renowned designer, manufacturer, and inventor of piano-making machinery. He learned the art of making pianos in Germany and came to NYC in 1874 and began importing piano parts. In 1874 he bought an old tannery site along E Canada Creek and began making felt which was prized worldwide for piano hammers. The next year

he bought 30,000 acres of forest nearby as the source for his sounding boards. The Village of Brockett's Bridge (renamed Dolgeville in 1887) grew from 300 to 2,000, mostly German immigrants.

A portion of the Village of Dolgeville is in the Town of Oppenheim. The East Canada Creek is the dividing line between Fulton County and Herkimer County. Dolgeville, which is primarily in Herkimer County, has several historic places, including part of the Alfred Dolge/Daniel Green properties on the east side of the creek. Building #1, where most of the manufacturing was located in the later years of the corporation, is in the Town of Oppenheim.

In 1881 Daniel Green, a traveling shoe salesman, visited Alfred Dolge's felt factory and saw workers wearing warm, felt slippers made from scraps of woolen piano felt. Daniel took a pair home to show his brother William in Canastota, NY. They asked Dolge if he would make the slippers for them and he agreed. In 1882 the Green brothers sold 600 pairs of slippers. Their sales mushroomed to 2,400 in 1883 and 24,000 in 1884. In 1885 felt heels were added to the slippers for outside use. Millions of slippers were made in Dolgeville before the factory closed in the 1990s after 120 years. The Daniel Green Company Factory Complex was added to the National Register of Historic Places in 1974.

POINTS OF INTEREST

Florence Jones Reineman Wildlife Sanctuary: Visit her sanctuary located a few miles north of Rt. 29, up the Belding Corners Rd. They have nature trails, and on Saturday nights in the summer they have programs, sometimes with live animals and even large reptiles. It is open

DATE: _____ WEATHER: _____

MEMORIES: _____

_____

_____

_____

_____

_____

_____

_____

_____

_____

_____ [Passport Stamp / Signature Here]

May thru September. 518-568-7101

Beaversprite Nature Center: Dorothy Richards, known as "Beaver Woman," studied beavers at Beaversprite Nature Center in Oppenheim for fifty years. She welcomed over 100,000 visitors to her house, where two consecutive beaver families lived in an addition, called the "Y." As part of her lifework to enlighten the public about this important, but shy, amphibious rodent, she wrote Beaversprite. She died in 1985. The Beaversprite Nature Center is open daily year-round by appointment. 141 Richards Rd., Dolgeville. Directions: From Dolgeville go 0.5 mile east on Rt. 29. Take 1st left on Sweet Hill Rd. Then go 40' and turn left on Lotville Rd. Go 2.3 miles and turn right on Richards Rd.

Daniel Green Company Factory Complex, South Main St., Dolgeville.

Camping:
Crystal Grove Campgrounds is located just south of Rt. 29, a mile or so west of Lassellsville, on Co. Rt. 114. You can go camping and also dig for diamonds, all in one place. The gemstones are crystals, called locally "Herkimer Diamonds" or "Little Falls Diamonds."

Material courtesy of Hector Allen, Town of Oppenheim Historian

This 1949 photo shows Dorothy Richards feeding tame beavers. Although she died in 1985, you may visit her home and learn about the beaver and its importance in nature. Allison M. Richards

65

STRATFORD

The most northwestern corner of Fulton County became the Town of Stratford on April 10, 1805. It was settled mostly by people from Stratford in Fairfield County, Connecticut, from whence it got its name. Stratford, consists of 49,156.28 acres and in 1890, the population was 997.

Stratford is in the southwestern Adirondack Park and has 12 lakes, 12 creeks and four small settlements: Stratford, Emmonsburg, Knappville, and Middlesprite.

In the 1800s, the town had eight one-room and one two-room schools. The schools became centralized in June 1928 and became one big central school erected in1930. This central school annexed with the Dolgeville Central School in 1984. The old central school in Stratford is still standing in the center of town but is in a state of disrepair and the site is used to store salvage vehicles, etc. The remaining small schools have either been demolished or made into family dwellings.

Some of the school uniforms, trophies, plaques, and yearbooks, which have been donated, occupy a locked cabinet in the Town Hall.

There are four cemeteries: Bliss on Avery Rd., Round Top on Rt. 29A, and Middlesprite and Mallett (the first burying place), all located on Co. Hwy. 119.

Lumbering and logging were the chief industries of early Stratford with 16 sawmills and five tanneries within the town. At the present time, none of these remain, but logging continues.

Other industries were cheesemaking and making butter tubs, sap buckets, clothes pins, and barrels.

David S. Watson was a wagon maker by trade but he invented a pressure jack, a glue table, and a pendant clothes dryer. In 1888, he received a patent on the Watson Dump wagon that he built in his barn in Stratford. Later he moved to Canastota to make his wagons and there is a museum with one.

There are remains of a Stone Pound on the corner of Stone Pound Rd. and Mallett Hill Rd. that at one time was used to hold stray pigs, cows, sheep, and horses, with a charge to get them out.

Stratford does have a snowmobile club and some groomed trails. A volunteer fire department is housed on Co. Rt. 104. Fishing and deer hunting are popular as Stratford consists of many acres of state land. One popular place to fish or put in a boat is Stewart Landing Dam on Stewart Landing Rd. (off Co. Hwy. 119). Some go for bullheads in evenings and families head there for swimming and picnics. There is some space for tents. The waterway can take you to Canada Lake by boat. East Canada Creek and Sprite Creek are good for trout.

INTERESTING PLACES TO VISIT

Visit cemeteries and the school items at the Town Hall, located at 120 Piseco Rd.

Music in the Gazebo: Usually in July, on Wednesday evenings at the Town Hall.

Annual Music Festival: Live music and food. At the Community Center attached to the Town Hall.

Material courtesy of Carolyn Walker, Town of Stratford Historian

DATE: _____ WEATHER: _____

MEMORIES: _____

_____

_____

_____

_____

_____

_____

_____

_____

_____

_____

_____

_____

_____

_____

[Passport Stamp / Signature Here]

David S. Watson invented the dump wagon in his barn in Stratford in the late 1800s. Carolyn Walker

WELLS

The Town of Wells is located in southern Hamilton County near Rt. 30. It is approx. 30 miles north of Gloversville in the southern Adirondack Mountains. The town includes the hamlet of Wells. The population in the 2010 census was 674.

HISTORY

In December 1769 Chief Hendricks of the Mohawk Indians took quill in hand and drew the picture of a turtle. That single act consummated a transaction to deed land on both sides of the Sacadaga River to John Bergen, Thomas Palmer, and 22 others. It marked the end of the Native American presence in their ancestral hunting grounds and the beginning of a new settlement that eventually became known as Wells.

Joshua Wells was an agent for Thomas Palmer when he and his wife settled the area. Much like the three rivers that converge at this location, so did other settlers, drawn by the waters that provided power for gristmills and sawmills, the foundation for any settlement to grow. By 1805 the population had grown to a point where essential services were required and the decision to form a township was made.

During much of its first 150 years, Wells was the center of commerce, finance, information, and politics within the county of Hamilton. But like many other rural areas at the turn of the 20th Century, Wells was finding itself more dependent on selling its natural beauty, not its natural resources.

The State of New York built the first state campground at the fork of the Main and West branches of the Sacandaga River and in 1925 the town dammed the Sacandaga River to form Lake Algonquin, all in an effort to attract tourists and second-home owners.

Today the State of New York owns in title or fee more than 90 percent of the land to be held as "forever wild" for the public's use. The 674 year-round residents and some 1500 seasonal residents seem comfortable with the more tranquil, laid-back role this grand old matriarch of Hamilton County towns now plays.

POINTS OF INTEREST

Algonquin Lake: This 3-mile-long lake along Rt. 30 provides swimming, boating, and fishing. It also has a public beach and a boat launch in the hamlet of Wells. There is also a municipal hydroelectric plant at the dam.

Auger Falls: (0.8 miles round trip) This 40-foot falls is at the beginning of a series of drops, plunges, and cascades totaling over 100 feet through this narrow gorge lined with hemlocks on the Sacandaga River.

Pine Orchard: The oldest stand of white pine in the State Forest Preserve. An easy walk for families to view mammoth "old growth" trees. Located off Dorr Rd.

Virginia Hosley Free Library: The Library caters to a wide variety of reader tastes providing books for all ages, puzzles, and videos. 1438 Rt. 30, Wells.

Wells Historical Museum: Open Summers. 1436 Rt. 30, Wells.

Material courtesy of Leona Aird, Town of Wells Historian & Brian Towers, Town Supervisor

DATE: _____ WEATHER: _____

MEMORIES: _____

_____

_____

_____

_____

_____

_____

_____

_____

_____

_____

_____

_____

_____

_____

[Passport Stamp / Signature Here]

During the early 1900s Lake Algonquin was created when a hydroelectric dam was built on the main branch of the Sacandaga River. The 3-mile-long lake along Rt. 30 provides swimming, boating, and fishing. Debbie Abbott-Forgione

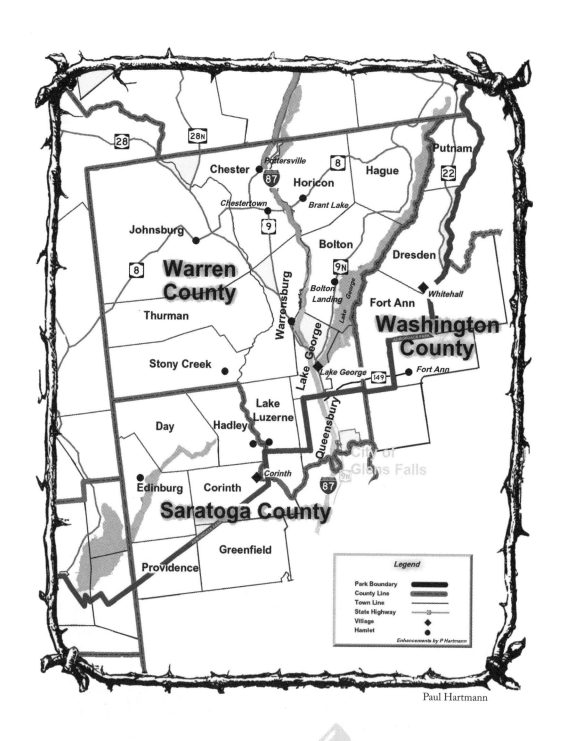

Paul Hartmann

CHAPTER 3

REGION III:

SARATOGA, WARREN & WASHINGTON COUNTIES

BOLTON

The Town of Bolton is located on the western shore of Lake George in the southeastern corner of the Adirondack Park.

HISTORY

The area that was to become Bolton was originally in the Town of Thurman in Washington County. In 1799 the New York Legislature created the Town of Bolton, and in 1813 the town became part of Warren County. Bolton's current boundaries were finally established in 1838. Bolton is the oldest town on Lake George and contains more than half of the lake's shoreline. The origins of the name Bolton have been lost in history, but it is reasonable to assume that the name came from either one of the New England Boltons or from one of the many English villages with Bolton in its name.

Most of Bolton's early settlers were Vermonters in search of farmland and opportunity. They cleared land well away from the lake and scraped together subsistence livings. Prior to the Civil War steamboats began to ply the waters of Lake George and several hamlets like The Huddle evolved on or near the shoreline. Bolton's first inn, The Mohican House, began to cater to lake travelers as the farm economy grew to include logging, making potash, low grade mining, and ice harvesting. After the Civil War an era of expansion occurred that brought hotels and large estates to the Bolton shoreline, and the hamlet of Bolton Landing grew to be the largest in the town. The agrarian economy shifted to an economy based on tourism. This expansion declined at the onset of World War I after Lake George's shoreline became known as Millionaire's Row.

By the end of World War II the era of motor courts and motels began to displace the old hotels and great estates of Bolton. The town's population never exceeded 2,000 people until the year 2000 census. Most of the town's property owners are now seasonal residents who cause the local population to swell some tenfold during the summer months. The hamlet of Bolton Landing has become a charming lakeside village offering a variety of cultural events, shops, restaurants, and lake related activities.

INTERESTING PLACES TO VISIT

Up Yonda Farm: Environmental education center on 73 acres. 5239 Lake Shore Dr., Bolton Landing. 518-644-9767, www.upyondafarm.com

The Sembrich Opera Museum: Museum tours and performances in a spectacular Lake George setting. 4800 Lake Shore Dr., Bolton Landing. 518-644-98339 (Museum), 518-644-24331 (Office), www.thesembrich.org

Rogers Memorial Park: Public beach, basketball court, tennis courts, public docks, picnic tables and grills, swings, steamboat, pier, and pavilion. 4928 Lake Shore Dr., Bolton Landing. 518-644-3831, www.boltonnewyork.com

Veterans Memorial Park: Public beach, basketball court, kayak launch, public docks, playground, picnic tables and grills and pavilion. 5034 Lake Shore Drive, Bolton Landing. 518-644-3831

Bolton Historical Museum: Local history museum. 4924 Lake Shore Dr., Bolton Landing. 518-644-99600, www.boltonhistorical.org

DATE: _____ WEATHER: _____

MEMORIES: _____

_____

_____

_____

_____

_____

_____

_____

_____

_____

_____

_____

_____

_____

_____

[Passport Stamp / Signature Here]

The Sagamore Hotel: A renovated Victorian-era hotel. 110 Sagamore Rd. 518-644-9400

Places to Hike:
Up Yonda Farm, Cat Mountain, Thomas Mountain, and Tongue Mountain Range.

Water Sports:
Canoe, kayak, and motorboat rentals at local marinas. Boat to islands and to any state lands bordering Lake George.

Material courtesy of Ted Caldwell, Bolton Historian & Michelle Huck, Recreation Director of Bolton

Bolton Historical Museum has many exhibits on the history of the region. Ted Caldwell

DAY

The Town of Day is in the northwest corner of Saratoga County and in the southeastern part of the Adirondack Park. It includes the hamlets of Day Center, Conklingville, and West Day. The town has land on both the east and west side of the Great Sacandaga Lake. The town population in 2010 was 856 people.

HISTORY

The Town of Day (originally named Concord) was formed in 1819 with land from the neighboring towns of Edinburg and Hadley. In the 19th Century the town was home to many industrial pursuits including lumbering, woodenware factories, tanneries and farming. The Sacandaga River ran through the center of town and hamlets such as Huntsville, Day Center and Conklingville grew up along its shores. In the early 1900s New York State built a dam across the Sacandaga River to control the terrible damage done each spring when the Hudson River flooded its banks. A small number of buildings were moved to higher ground and remain standing today.

The Conklingville Dam was completed in 1930 and the character of Day was changed forever. The town became a vacation community. People built seasonal camps along the shores of the newly created Great Sacandaga Lake and came to enjoy the beauty of its surrounding mountain views and quiet wilderness. Day has continued to preserve its rural character into the 21st Century and is still a popular tourist destination in all seasons.

INTERESTING PLACES TO VISIT

The Town Park is on the shores of the Great Sacandaga Lake. There are picnic tables and grills on the grounds for public use. The park is located along North Shore Road near the eastern boundary of the town.

Places to Hike, Canoe, Etc:
The Great Sacandaga Lake is a beautiful place to swim, fish, canoe, sail, or motorboat. You can launch your watercraft for free at the Saratoga County Boat Launch on North Shore Rd. In the winter snowmobiling and ice fishing are very popular on the Great Sacandaga Lake.

Historic Sites:
The Town of Day Museum at 1650 North Shore Road. The museum is open on Saturdays from 10 am – 1 pm in July and August in the former Town Hall, which was built in the 1930s by the Works Progress Administration. The museum's collection includes historic photographs, antique farming equipment, items related to the building of the Conklingville Dam and information on some of the town's prominent residents.

Material courtesy of Lauren Roberts, Town of Day Historian

DATE: _____ WEATHER: _____

MEMORIES: _____

_____

_____

_____

_____

_____

_____

_____

_____

_____

_____

_____

_____

_____

_____

[Passport Stamp / Signature Here]

The construction of the Conklingville Dam. Lauren Roberts

CHESTER

The Town of Chester is located in Warren County, near the southeastern corner of the Adirondack Park, along Rt. 9 and north of Warrensburg. It includes the following villages and hamlets: Chestertown, Darrowsville, Pottersville, and Igerna. It also includes Loon, Brant, and Friends lakes.

Chester was first settled about 1794. It was set off from the Town of Thurman in 1799. The town has several sites associated with the Underground Railroad. In 1964 Chester donated the National Christmas Tree to the White House.

POINTS OF INTEREST

Darrowsville Cemetery: Located on Dennehy Road about 2.5 miles south of Chestertown. Adjacent to the cemetery was the Darrowsville Wesleyan Methodist Church. It was built in 1845 and was a stop on the Underground Railroad. The abolitionist minister Thomas Baker and his wife are buried there.

Chester Rural Cemetery: Just south of Chestertown. As you enter, on the left you'll see an old Quaker burial ground. On the far right nearest Rt. 9 is the grave of John Butler Yeats, an Irish painter and writer, and father of poet William Butler Yeats.

Town of Chester Municipal Center: Located at 6307 Rt. 9, Chestertown. On the second floor is the Town of Chester Library and the Local Museum, which is operated by the Town of Chester Historical Society. www.townofchesterny.org

Chester Historic District: Three buildings in Chestertown are on the National Register of Historic Places.

Main Street Ice Cream Parlor: This excellent restaurant, soda fountain, and gift store is in the restored 1913 school. 6339 Main St., Chestertown. www.mainstreeticecreamparlor.com

The Church of the Good Shepherd: Built in 1884 for $2,500. Main St., Chestertown.

Chester Inn: Built in the early 1800s is a bed and breakfast. 6347 Main St., Chestertown. www.thechesterinn.com

Railroads on Parade: A model train museum with wonderful, ever-changing moving displays. 7903 Rt. 9, Pottersville. www.railroadsonparade.com

Natural Stone Bridge & Caves: Morse's Geography of 1790 gives the first description of the caves. It has the largest marble cave entrance in the East. 535 Stone Bridge Rd., Pottersville. www.stonebridgeandcaves.com

The Crossroads Country Store: It has all you need for outdoor sports such as hunting, fishing, and camping, plus groceries, sandwiches, gifts, clothing, and books. 40 Dixon Rd., Chestertown.

RECREATION

Dynamite Hill Recreation Area: A small (65' drop!) rope-tow area that operates in Chestertown just off Rt. 8. The town purchased the property in 1962 and developed a skiing area, a sledding hill, a ball diamond, and a picnic area. It is run by the Rotary Club and skiing is free.

Caroline Fish Memorial Crosscountry Trail: From the stoplight in Chestertown head north to Landon Hill Road. Along this road you'll

DATE: _____ WEATHER: _____

MEMORIES: _____

_____

_____

_____

_____

_____

_____

_____

_____

_____

_____

_____

_____

_____

[Passport Stamp / Signature Here]

find the ski trail and the site of the 1964 National Christmas Tree.

Scaroon Manor Campground and Day Use Area: Located on Rt. 9 north of Pottersville. This was the site of the former luxury resort, Scaroon Manor, where the classic movie "Marjorie Morningstar" starring Natalie Wood and Gene Kelly was filmed. www.dec.ny.gov/outdoor/72082.html

Material courtesy of Donna Lagoy, Town of Chester Historian

The 1913 Union School on 6339 Main St. in Chestertown that is now the home of Main Street Ice Cream Parlor. Donna Lagoy

77

CORINTH TOWN & VILLAGE

The Town of Corinth is known as the "Gateway to the Adirondacks" and is situated in the northern portion of Saratoga County. It includes the Village of Corinth and the following hamlets: Palmer, Randall Corners, and South Corinth. There are also five lakes: Efner, Hunt, Jenny, Bonita, and Woodland.

The Hudson River carved out the palisades above Palmer Falls. Pagenstecher Park, located in the village of Corinth, offers an excellent view of this natural feature.

HISTORY

The area was a lush hunting and fishing site for the Native Americans, but the bountiful timber is what attracted the Jessup Brothers to harvest the logs of the southern Adirondacks. The timber was tied together as rafts and sent down the river to sawmills for export to England in the mid-1700s. The Revolutionary War caused the British Loyalists to flee to Canada and left the area open to settlement by numerous New England families seeking more land.

The Hudson River as well as several small creeks provided ample water power for gristmills and sawmills. A woolen mill and edge tool factory preceded the establishment of the Hudson River Pulp and Paper Company which in 1898 joined forces with 17 other northeast paper mills to become International Paper Company. This mill which at one time was the largest paper mill in the country closed its doors in 2002 and now nearly all the buildings have been demolished in the village of Corinth. See more information about the mill at www.hudsonrivermillproject.org.

POINTS OF INTEREST

Corinth Museum: Open on Saturdays from 1 pm – 3 pm. An active Corinth Museum Facebook page displays hundreds of photographs from the museum collection. 609 Palmer Ave., Corinth.

Saratoga North Creek Railroad: Stops at the Corinth station. Head out of the village on Hamilton Ave., and turn right just before the railroad underpass. Wait for a train and it will stop. www.sncrr.com

Access to the Hudson River: In the village, above Palmer Falls and also at Clothier Hollow along Co. Rt. 24 (near the intersection with Folts Rd., above the Spier Falls Dam).

Jessup's Landing Pathway is a paved walkway along the Hudson River with two picnic areas. It begins behind the Corinth Free Library at the beach and continues to Pagenstecher Park behind the Presbyterian Church on Palmer Ave.

A public beach is located near the Corinth Free Library and is open during the summer.

Corinth Free Library: Be sure to visit this library! It offers programs and services to all ages. 89 Main St., Corinth.

Corinth is the "Snowshoe Capital of the World" and ice fishing is popular on the Hudson River. The town website, www.corinthny.com, has more details about recreation in the area. The village offers a variety of shops and eateries along Main St., Palmer Ave., and the surrounding areas.

Material courtesy of Rachel Clothier, Town of Corinth Historian

DATE: _____ WEATHER: _____

MEMORIES: _____

_____

_____

_____

_____

_____

_____

_____

_____

_____

_____

_____

_____

_____

_____

[Passport Stamp / Signature Here]

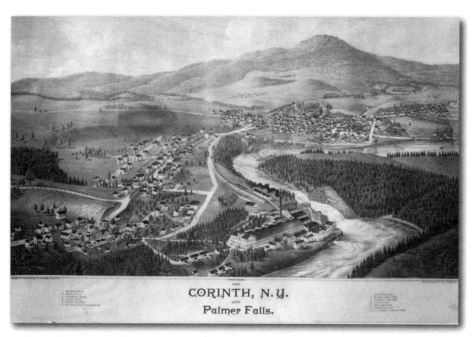

A bird's eye view of Corinth in 1888. The large mill in the lower right would later become the International Paper Company, the largest paper mill in the country.
Rachel Clothier

DRESDEN

The Town of Dresden is in the northern section of Washington County and the southeastern part of the Adirondack Park. The town contains these hamlets: Clemons, Dresden, Huletts Landing, and Dresden Station. Dresden was originally part of the Town of Westfield. One of the first settlers, Joseph Phippeny arrived in 1784. It officially became the Town of Dresden in 1823.

Dresden is one of those glorious places that boasts so many natural attributes it's hard to determine where to start. Wholly inside the Adirondack Park, it has the majestic Lake George on its west side and Lake Champlain on the eastern border. On the southern border is South Bay, which consists of the headwaters of Lake Champlain, or make your way north to where Dresden is bordered by the town of Putnam. Hiking up Black Mountain (2646'), one can follow an 8.5-mile trail to the top of the highest mountain above Lake George. Here you can get breathtaking views of the northern part of Lake George. There is also the Black Mountain fire tower that is now used as a communication tower.

One first crosses into Dresden at South Bay. Here is a state boat launch which allows access to Lake Champlain. Rt. 22 bisects the town with Co. Rt. 6 to the left heading to the hamlet of Huletts Landing and the county beach on Lake George, and right to town center and the hamlet of Clemons. While summer tourism and seasonal residents enjoy this pristine part of Lake George, the population of the entire town of Dresden hasn't changed much since the 1870 census. Then it was 684 and the 2000 census indicated a population of 677. It covers 55 square miles, with a population density of 12.7 people per square mile. It is one of the

Adirondack's best kept secrets. Once you've been here, you'll know that though there are no street lights, grocery stores, or gas stations, Dresden has a big heart. The town can rally together to help one of its own at a moments' notice.

History whispers in all corners of town. On June 28, 1756 Captain Rogers left Fort William Henry with 50 of his rangers, in five whale boats, on a mission to reconnoiter Fort Carillon (Ticonderoga) and parts of Lake Champlain, which was controlled by the French. They traveled up Lake George and spent the first night on one of the islands in the lake. The next day, June 29th, they arrived in the area of Huletts Landing. From there they took the five whale boats up and over the mountains of the Town of Dresden, to Lake Champlain. . ." This is commemorated by two historic marker signs at the rest area on Rt. 22, and the other at the Washington County Park in Huletts Landing.

So whether you seek history, natural scenic vistas, pristine lakes, or traveling the length of some of the most beautiful lakes that New York has to offer, Dresden is the place.

Material courtesy of Kathy Huntington, Dresden Town Historian

DATE: _____ WEATHER: _____

MEMORIES: _____

_____

_____

_____

_____

_____

_____

_____

_____

_____

_____

_____

_____

_____

_____

_____

_____

[Passport Stamp / Signature Here]

A view from Rt. 22 looking west at the headwaters of Lake Champlain as you cross the bridge from Whitehall into the Town of Dresden. Kathy Huntington

EDINBURG

The Town of Edinburg is tucked away in the northwestern part of Saratoga County in the foothills of the Adirondack Mountains. The town is situated on both the east and western side of the Great Sacandaga Lake.

Edinburg's location and people played an important role in New York history. Settlers arrived in the Sacandaga River Valley in 1787. Veteran Abijah Stark came from Massachusetts and settled just north of Fish House. He was followed by many other families. Folks came for the virgin pine forests, fertile lands, and "elbow room."

Originally part of the Town of Providence, settlers decided to hold an informal meeting naming the town Northfield in 1801. In 1808 the town was renamed Edinburg because another Northfield was discovered in New York State.

As growth continued, Edinburg was distinguished by several communities including Beecher Hollow and Tennantville on the west and Batchellerville on the east side of the Sacandaga Valley. These communities had their own schoolhouses and cemeteries. Today, the Beecher Hollow School is home to the Nellie Tyrrell Museum depicting much of Edinburg's vibrant history. It is next to the Edinburg Fire House at 7 North Shore Rd.

Farming, logging, and woodenware manufacturing drew large industries to Edinburg. Batchellerville became a manufacturing community having several large woodenware mills. Beecher Hollow was more farming-oriented. These two areas had large sawmills and woodenware mills, most of which have since burned.

Propelled by the Abolitionist Movement, Edinburg citizens helped run-away slaves find freedom using the Underground Railroad. Edinburg is home to one of the most distinguished stops, known as Barker's store. Visitors can still view a small hiding space that harbored many on their road to freedom. Barker's store is located at the corner of Military and North Shore Road.

Like the settlers before him, Edinburg resident Arad Copeland built his own home and the only covered bridge still standing in Saratoga County in 1879. Visitors can enjoy the Copeland Covered Bridge in the summer and fall. Parking is available along North Shore Road, Co. Rt. 4

Seeking jobs after the mills burned many residents moved out of Edinburg. Later, the Conklingville Dam was built at the edge of the Valley and the Valley was flooded. On March 27, 1930 the gates on the Conklingville Dam were closed and by 1931 the Valley was lost forever as the Great Sacandaga Lake was created.

Today the shores of the Great Sacandaga Lake are dotted with hundreds of seasonal homes creating a mecca for seasonal fun. Fishing, hiking, boating, ice fishing, and snowmobiling remain family fun events for everyone in Edinburg. Life has changed in Edinburg, but the people haven't.

Material courtesy of Priscilla L. Edwards, Town of Edinburg Historian & Maria Spaeth, Assistant Historian

DATE: _____ WEATHER: _____

MEMORIES: _____

_____

_____

_____

_____

_____

_____

_____

_____

_____

_____

_____

_____

_____

_____

_____

[Passport Stamp / Signature Here]

Barker's Store (1847), located at the corner of Military and North Shore
Road, was one of the important stops on the Underground Railroad.
Priscilla L. Edwards

FORT ANN

The Town of Fort Ann, NE of Glens Falls, lies between Lake Champlain and Lake George in Washington Co. The town is contains these hamlets and villages: West Fort Ann, Comstock, South Bay Village, Needhamville, Hog Town, and Welch Hollow.

The town is rich in military history. It had one of five forts built by the British in 1755 to protect against a French invasion. The fort was named in honor of Princess Anne, eldest daughter of King George II of England. Fort Ann was located on present-day Rt. 4 and midway between Half Way Brook and Wood Creek. During the American Revolution the Patriots gained control of Fort Ann. At the Battle of Fort Ann on July 8, 1777, the Patriots helped slow down Burgoyne's British troops on their way from Ticonderoga to Saratoga. This battle resulted in the Americans beating Burgoyne in Saratoga.

In 1927 a plaque was placed at the base of Battle Hill near the fort to honor that battle. A replica of the fort was built and placed at the original site in the 1950s and now houses Glens Falls National Bank. A park was built on the opposite side of the road from the fort and just south of Battle Hill. People can have picnics and a kiosk has brochures of the Town of Fort Ann.

One of the wells used by the fort is still available to visit. A historical marker can be found as you go north from the village at the corner of Rt. 4 and Co. Rt. 16.

Fort Ann had many industries. There was a knitting mill at Kanes Falls. The mill was built near an old waterfall about a mile north of Fort Ann. There were many sawmills, gristmills, and farms in Fort Ann. The mills are gone but farming continues to prosper.

There are 489 known Veterans buried throughout the Town of Fort Ann from every war starting with the French and Indian War to the present.

INTERESTING PLACES

Champlain Canal runs through Fort Ann. There is a little park with a gazebo on Clay Hill just off the intersection of Rts. 149 & 4 where can you watch the boats go by and see the old canal locks.

Fort Ann Historical Society at the Old Stone Library on 53 George St. in Fort Ann, has a walking tour brochure that is available at the bank, post office, and town hall.

Buttermilk Falls: Follow Rt. 149 east towards Fort Ann from Lake George for 1.6 miles to the intersection of Rts. 149 and 9. Take a left onto Buttermilk Falls Rd. and go 3 miles until it becomes Sly Pond Road (unpaved). At 8.7 miles the name changes again to Shelving Rock Road. Look for a large parking lot on the right. There are hiking trails to Buttermilk Falls, and Sleeping Beauty, Black, and Buck mountains.

Country Meadows Golf Course: 14 holes at 10786 Rt. 149, Fort Ann.

Harris Airport: Features plane and helicopter scenic tours and sky-diving. 10913 Rt. 149, Fort Ann.

Hill Billy Fun Park: Miniature golf and ice cream. 10375 Rt. 149, Fort Ann.

Fort Ann was a military town, a canal town, an industrial town, and a farming town. Today Fort Ann still has farming and is a small quiet

DATE: _____ WEATHER: _____

MEMORIES: _____

_____

_____

_____

_____

_____

_____

_____

_____

_____

_____

_____

_____

_____

[Passport Stamp / Signature Here]

rural town sitting at the foothills of the Adirondacks.

Material courtesy of Virginia Parrott, Town of Fort Ann Historian

The Fort Ann Post of the Glens Falls National Bank is a replica of the actual fort that once stood on the site. Carolyn & Gene Ouderkirk

85

GREENFIELD

The historic Town of Greenfield is situated in the southern foothills of the Adirondack Mountains a short distance northwest of Saratoga Springs. It is composed of these hamlets: Chatfield Corner, Greenfield, Greenfield Center, Middle Grove, Kings, North Greenfield, Pages Corner, and Porter Corners.

The Kayaderosseras Creek has its headwaters in the northern section of the town and flows south through the town providing excellent trout fishing. The town lies mostly within the Kayaderosseras Patent, a large land purchase contract between the Queen of England and the Mohawk Indians concluded in 1761.

Most of the first settlers arrived shortly after the Revolutionary War and promptly cleared the forest creating many small farms. Most of the farms were allowed to return to forest resulting in a brisk lumbering business. However, because of its proximity to the Capital District via the Northway, the town of between 7,000 and 8,000 inhabitants is now primarily residential.

The original town (formed in 1793) was much larger and included what are now several townships to the north. In 1801, it was reduced to near its present size, but is still the largest township in Saratoga County covering nearly 68 square miles.

POINTS OF INTEREST

Lake Desolation: Along the western border of the town is a beautiful small spring-fed lake on top of a mountain.

Museum at the historic Odd Fellows Hall. 430 Middle Grove Rd., Middle Grove.

Stone Bank in Porter Corners, which is reputed to be one of the oldest bank buildings in Saratoga County. Co. Rt. 19, N. Creek Rd.

Castle-like stone and concrete Graphite Mill ruins in the deep woods on the mountainside above Porter Corners which can be accessed by a 45-minute moderately steep hike.

Historic Mansion on the hill in Greenfield Center.

Brookhaven Golf Course: A scenic 18-hole course nestled in the foothills of the Kayaderosseras Range. 333 Alpine Meadows Rd., Porter Corners.

Stewart's Ice Cream Plant: On historic Rt. 9N, once a plank road, is home of NY state's best milk and the world's best ice cream. 461 Church St.

Material courtesy of Ron Feulner, Town of Greenfield Historian

DATE: _____ WEATHER: _____

MEMORIES: _____

_____

_____

_____

_____

_____

_____

_____

_____

_____

_____

_____

_____

_____

_____

_____

_____

[Passport Stamp / Signature Here]

The Stone Bank located on Co. Rt. 19 on N. Creek Rd. in Porter Corners
is one of the oldest bank buildings in Saratoga. Ron Feulner

HADLEY

The Town of Hadley is located in the northeast corner of Saratoga County, at the confluence of the Hudson and Sacandaga rivers. Its total area is 41.1 square miles. It is one of three towns in Saratoga County located entirely in the Adirondack Park.

HISTORY

The Town of Hadley originated Feb. 27, 1801 from the towns of Greenfield and Northumberland. The town of Corinth was removed in 1818 and a section of the Town of Day in 1819. In the early 1930s, the Conklingville Dam was built in the Town of Hadley to form the Great Sacandaga Lake to control flooding along the Hudson River. In 1958 a second dam was built, about a mile downstream from the first, creating Stewarts Pond. Both of these dams today are used for downstream flood control and also for hydro-electric generation. The stretch of river between the second dam and the Hudson River is used for recreational rafting, tubing and kayaking on some of the only dam controlled white water in New York State.

POINTS OF INTEREST

Hadley Fire Tower is a great hike for the entire family. The state built a 40' steel tower on Hadley Mt. and it became operational in 1917. It closed in 1990 but was restored by the Hadley Fire Tower Committee. Each summer, there is a summit guide that tells the history of the tower. Directions: From the village of Hadley travel N on Rt. 9N and turn right on Stony Creek Rd. After traveling 3 miles, bear left on Hadley Hill Rd. and go 4.5 miles. Turn right on Tower Rd. and proceed 1.5 miles to the trailhead parking lot.

For the water enthusiast, there is a wide variety of opportunities. You can go whitewater rafting, tubing, or kayaking on the Sacandaga River. Enjoy the wild Hudson River in your paddle boats, canoes, kayaks, or tubes above the famed Rockwell Falls or enjoy the power boat opportunities below the falls. There are also great hunting and fishing opportunities throughout the town.

Hadley is home to a quaint and challenging Bend of the River Golf Club 9-hole golf course. 5 Park Ave., Hadley.

There is a train station for the Saratoga North Creek Railway that offers spectacular scenic views along the Hudson River valley. 4209 Rockwell St., Hadley.

Historic Places:
These include the fire tower and also the historic Bow Bridge. The Bow Bridge was built in 1885 replacing a burned covered bridge that was built in 1813. The parabolic Bow Bridge was one of three iron lenticular truss bridges built in New York State and the only one still standing. The Bow Bridge was placed on the National Historic Register on March 25, 1977. It was refurbished and reopened to traffic in 2008 and is still in use as a one lane bridge today. While visiting the Bow Bridge you will also see the train trestle that carries the scenic Saratoga North Creek Train over the Sacandaga river 100 feet in the air (Old Corinth Road).

Dining & Shopping:
The hamlet of Hadley offers a few pubs and restaurants and also a general store. There are many lodging and other dining opportunities located just across the river in Lake Luzerne. Hadley is a unique little town

DATE: _____ WEATHER: _____

MEMORIES: _____

_____

_____

_____

_____

_____

_____

_____

_____

_____

_____

_____

_____

_____

[Passport Stamp / Signature Here]

that shares a lot of services with Lake Luzerne including schools, the fire department, ambulance squad, a library, and a museum. Lynnwood is another hamlet in the west part of the town at the junction of Co. Rds. 7 & 8.

Hadley offers a wide range of recreational and cultural opportunities and is located close enough to Lake George and Saratoga to make a day trip to Hadley enjoyable for the whole family.

Material courtesy of Arthur "Mo" Wright, Town of Hadley Supervisor

This 1885 parabolic Bow Bridge crosses the Sacandaga River near Old Corinth Rd. It replaced an 1813 covered bridge that burned. Maureen Lanfear

HAGUE

The Town of Hague is located at the Intersection of Rts. 9N and 8 in northern Warren County. It is approx. 8 miles south of Ticonderoga and includes the hamlets of Hague, Graphite, Silver Bay, Sabbath Day Point, and Indian Kettles.

The Town of Hague is an enticing community on the shores of Lake George, America's Queen of Lakes.

Hague has long been a draw for settlers, tourists, and travelers. Many early settlers came here from Massachusetts and Vermont and made their living as hardscrabble farmers, innkeepers, lumbermen, tanners, and fishing, and hunting guides. By the late 1800s Hague's shores were dotted with substantial hotels and guest houses. Thus began the "heyday" of hotels with guests arriving by steamboat from the head of the lake at Caldwell. Toting their trunks, people came to spend the summer and found a warm welcome. Tables were laden with fresh produce from local farms and trout dinners abounded daily. Some of these hotels are still welcoming guests in the 21st Century.

After the 1920s the roads opened and visitors could now come by automobile. Initially it was a pretty bumpy road but the highway improved and the motoring public began to arrive looking for a new kind of accommodations. This began the era of cottage colonies and camping facilities. What remained the same was the allure of the lake and the mountains.

The hotels and tourist facilities provided work for the local population. Farmers had outlets for their products and over the years other industries added to employment opportunities. The discovery of graphite in Hague's hillsides supported a mining industry for some years.

The Hacker Boat Company still produces a premier line of pleasure craft here and Hague is home to the Silver Bay YMCA of the Adirondacks.

Hague has had a colorful history and is still a great place to while away summer hours as well as being close to facilities for winter sports. Come and visit us!

INTERESTING PLACES TO VISIT

Town Park includes a beach and boat launch. Also has summer music in the park program during July & August, Wednesdays at 7:30 pm.

Rogers Rock State Park has 332 campsites, beach, showers, etc. Popular activities there include boating, fishing, swimming, bicycling, and hiking. 9894 Lake Shore Dr.

Silver Bay YMCA of the Adirondacks: a conference center founded in 1900. 87 Silver Bay Rd., Silver Bay. www.silverbay.org

Places to Hike, Canoe, Etc:
Lake George, North Pond, Rogers Rock State Park, Jabez Pond, 5 Mile Mountain, Deer Leap, Berry Mill Pond. www.townofhague.org

Historic Sites to Visit:
Hague Historical Museum. Open Monday thru Friday, 8:30 am – 4 pm. 9793 Graphite Mountain Rd., Hague. 518-543-6161

Fort Ticonderoga. 30 Ft. Ti Rd., Ticonderoga.

Hancock House. Open all year, Moses Circle, Ticonderoga. 518-585-7868

Material courtesy of Pat McDonough, Hague Historical Society

DATE: _____ WEATHER: _____

MEMORIES: _____

_____

_____

_____

_____

_____

_____

_____

_____

_____

_____

_____

_____

_____

_____

_____

[Passport Stamp / Signature Here]

The downtown shopping area of Hague on Rt. 8 near the
intersection of Rt. 9N (near Lake George). Pat McDonough

91

HORICON

The Town of Horicon is located in the northeastern corner of Warren County. The town has three hamlets: Brant Lake, South Horicon, and Adirondack.

HISTORY

Horicon was settled in the early 1800s and incorporated March 29, 1838 from portions of Bolton and Hague, with a total of 71.8 square miles. During the Civil War, the town held the proud distinction of providing more volunteer soldiers in proportion to the population than any other town in NYS with only one man being drafted.

The tanning industry was important to the area. There were tanneries in Adirondack and one of the largest in New York State was in South Horicon. Hides were brought by railroad to Riverside and transported by wagons or by steam ships to South Horicon. The hemlock bark needed to tan the hides was cut thoroughout the area, but especially in the Pharaoh Lake Wilderness area.

By the mid-1880s the tourism business began to spring up with guest houses and hotels. Many families lived by subsistence farming.

INTERESTING PLACES

Brant Lake, Schroon Lake, Schroon River, and a myriad of quiet ponds and creeks are accessible by public boat launches and winding country roads. The picturesque Mill Pond in Brant Lake is the perfect spot for a stroll or to fish from the pier.

Horicon Museum: A look into the past: early settlers, their homes, churches, industries, boarding houses, celebrations. It is a nine-room restored 19th Century farmhouse that displays

many photographs of the spectacular and beautiful scenery in this Adirondack region, as well as artifacts from early homes and businesses. Open June-August, free admission. 6696 Rt. 8, Brant Lake. 518-494-7286

Recreation:
Lily Pond and Pharaoh Lake: Hike, snowshoe, and cross-country ski.

Brant Lake, Schroon Lake, and Schroon River: Boat, canoe, kayak, swim, bike, and fish. Public beaches and boat launches.

Ridin-Hy Ranch Resort: Rodeo, horseback riding, downhill skiing & tubing, restaurant, indoor pool, boating, swimming, fishing. 95 N Sherman Lake Rd., Ridin Highway Ranch Rd., Warrensburg. www.ridinhy.com

Tin TeePee Campground: 144 Bean Rd., Brant Lake. www.tinteepeecampground.com

Historic Sites:
Veterans Memorial Monuments: History sweeps from the walkway at 6604 Rt. 8 Brant Lake. Take a break in the park and enjoy the view. Located on East Shore Dr., Adirondack.

Adirondack Schoolhouse: Built in the early 1900s, it is still standing and is now the site of the Adirondack Community Center and Horicon Volunteer Fire Department annex. The schoolhouse looks the same as it did a century ago. The bell from the first schoolhouse, built in 1852, is displayed.

Hienzelman Library: Built in the early 1900s, it still remains on the shore of the Mill Pond in Brant Lake. The one-story stone building which housed the public library for over 90 years is now a historical library and the Town Historian's office.

DATE: _____ WEATHER: _____

MEMORIES: _____

_____

_____

_____

_____

_____

_____

_____

_____

_____

_____

[Passport Stamp / Signature Here]

Local Businesses:
Adirondack General Store: Groceries, gifts, and books. 899 East Shore Dr., Adirondack. 518-494-4408, www.adkgeneralstore.com

The Lazy Moose and Garden Market: Garden store, general store, café, and gifts. 6699 Rt. 8 Brant Lake. 518-494-4039, thelazymoosegardenmarket.com

The Hub: Bicycle repair shop and café. 27 Market St., Brant Lake. 518-494-4822

Suzy Q's Restaurant: 142 Tannery Rd., Brant Lake. 518-494-4381

Jimbo's Club at the Pointe: 7201 Rt. 8, Brant Lake. www.jimbosclub.com

Palmer Brothers Marina: 33 Palisades Rd., Brant Lake. 518-494-2677

EZ Marine and Storage: 11 Town Shed Rd., Brant Lake. 518-494-7381

Clark's Country Mall Farmer's Market: 6752 Rt. 8, Brant Lake.

Material courtesy of Sylvia Smith, Town of Horicon Councilwoman & Christine Hayes, Town Assessor

The Horicon Museum is at 6696 Rt. 8 in Brant Lake. Sylvia Smith

93

JOHNSBURG

The Town of Johnsburg is in the northwest corner of Warren County. Within Johnsburg there are nine hamlets: Bakers Mills, Johnsburg, North Creek, North River, Riparius, Wevertown, Sodom, The Glen, and Garnet Lake.

In 1788 NYS sold John Thurman, a wealthy New York City merchant, 25,200 acres of Township #12 of the Totten and Crossfield Purchase. The first clearing took place about 1790 on Elm Hill, located one mile south of today's hamlet of Johnsburg. This name was taken from Thurman's first name and was spelled Johnsburgh until 1893. It was partitioned from the original Town of Thurman on April 6, 1805.

Land was cleared along Beaver Brook (now called Mill Creek), and a gristmill and sawmill were erected at the falls of the brook. A distillery was opened which produced a market for rye. In 1795 a woolen factory was built, but was converted to a cotton factory two years later. Thurman erected his Calico printing works, one of the first in America. He also built ash works and made large quantities of pot ash. Farmers were paid one shilling per bushel for ashes.

Joseph Hopper kept the first tavern, one of the places chosen for annual town meetings and elections. John Richards was elected the first town supervisor, a position he held several times afterwards. Robert Waddell operated Thurman's store at Elm Hill and conducted business dealings for him, because John Thurman often traveled to the shipping ports of London and New York.

On Sept. 27, 1809 Thurman was run through and killed by an enraged bull in Bolton. He

was 79 years old. John Thurman is buried inside a cut-stone enclosure within the Wevertown Cemetery on Rt. 28.

From 1832 until the 1890s there were tanneries that provided many jobs. Logging made the lumbering industry thrive between North River and Glens Falls by using the Hudson River for river drives. Several streams were dammed by area men taking advantage of water power for operating sawmills and gristmills. With the arrival of the railroad in 1871, transportation was revolutionized, and North Creek developed into the hub of our town with its ever-growing businesses. Garnet mining continues today by the Barton Mines Corp., our longest operating family-owned industry since 1878.

By 1894 there were 21 rural school districts through the eighth grade. The first high school was built in 1898 in North Creek. Today's Johnsburg Central School offers an excellent education to about 430 students in grades K-12.

In North Creek you can walk to restaurants, shopping, hotels, motels, and B&B's.

INTERESTING PLACES TO VISIT

Gore Mountain Ski Center: 103 trails, 2,537 vertical feet, and 15 lifts including a high-speed eight-passenger Northwoods Gondola. 793 Peaceful Valley Rd., North Creek. www.goremountain.com

Saratoga North Creek Railroad: Passenger service between Saratoga & North Creek by the scenic Hudson River. 3 Railroad Pl., North Creek. www.sncrr.com

Tannery Pond Community Center: A multi-

DATE: _____ WEATHER: _____

MEMORIES: _____

_____

_____

_____

_____

_____

_____

_____

_____

_____

_____

_____

_____

_____

[Passport Stamp / Signature Here]

purpose building containing meeting rooms, gallery, and auditorium. Main St., North Creek. www.tpcca.org

Little Gore: Winter fun park to ski, snowboard, and tube under lights. The Hudson Chair provides access to the rest of Gore's slopes. Located off Rt. 28.

North Creek Railroad Depot Museum: Main St., North Creek. www.sncrr.com

Johnsburg Historical Society: P.O. Box 144, Wevertown. Open Mondays, 9 am – 1 pm. 518-251-5788

Material courtesy of Jo Ann Smith, Johnsburg Town Clerk

A 1913 postcard of the D & H Railroad Station in North Creek. Jo Ann Smith

LAKE GEORGE TOWN & VILLAGE

The Town of Lake George is north of Glens Falls in the southeastern Adirondacks. The Town of Lake George is composed of the Village of Lake George and the hamlets of Big Hollow, Crosbyside, and Diamond Point. It is located between exits 20 and 23 of the Adirondack Northway (I-87).

Lake George, formerly called "Caldwell," was formed on Aug. 2, 1810. It is the smallest town in Warren County (32 square miles), originally named for James Caldwell and renamed as "Lake George" in 1962.

The entire region is rich in history, and the town sits on one of the most pristine bodies of water in the world. Lake George was originally called "Andia-ta-roc-te" by the Native Americans and was later named "Lac du St. Sacrament" by Father Isaac Joques, the first white man to see the lake in 1646. The lake was finally named "Lake George" by Sir William Johnson in 1755 for King George II of England.

Lake George was a strategic battleground in the Seven Years War, known as the "French and Indian War." Here, Montcalm fought against Amherst and Abercrombie. Later, Ethan Allen and his Green Mountain Boys and Burgoyne, Benedict Arnold and his Canadian force, as well as the Native Americans, battled on and along the shores of Lake George.

Lake George at one time had three forts: Fort Gage, Fort George, and Fort William Henry. Fort George was built by General Amherst in 1759. It was never completed but was used as a base of operations from which to attack Fort Ticonderoga, 32 miles north at the north end of the lake. Fort William Henry was

built in 1755 and was burned in 1757 by the French; Native American forces and General Montcalm forced the occupants under General Monroe to surrender. The fort was rebuilt in 1953 and exists today as a replica.

Bloody Pond was the site of the battle between Dieskau's forces and Colonial reinforcements. After surrounding the French, the provincials opened fire and the dead were thrown in the pond. The water became red with blood, and since Sept. 8, 1755, it has been known as "Bloody Pond."

By the late 1800s, the Village of Lake George was beginning to grow, primarily because of its beauty and the lake. The main business was lumbering. Then came steamboats on the lake and the D&H Railroad, marking the beginning of the tourist trade. Wealthy people bought homes along Rt. 9N, Bolton Road, and the eastern shore of Lake George.

ACTIVITIES

Today, Lake George plays host to thousands of summer tourists from May to October. Winter is also a great time to visit. Winter Carnival, weekends in February, and there's plenty of skiing nearby.

Boat Cruises: Lake George Shoreline Cruises (2 Kurosaka Ln.) and Lake George Steamboat Company (57 Beach Rd.).

There are many trails to hike, or drive to the top of Prospect Mountain for incredible views.

Get a taste of our rich history at Fort William Henry (48 Canada St.) and Lake George Historical Association Museum (290 Canada St.).

96

DATE: _____ WEATHER: _____

MEMORIES: _____

_____

_____

_____

_____

_____

_____

_____

_____

_____

_____

_____

_____

_____

[Passport Stamp / Signature Here]

We have beautiful beaches and a bike trail that starts at the head of the lake and winds 10 miles south to Glens Falls. Play mini-golf, have an ice cream cone, or simply take a stroll through the village and down the lakefront boardwalk.

Plan to stop by the Visitor Information Center at One Beach Road before visiting our shops and parks. Also, these websites will help you plan your trip:

www.lakegeorge.com
www.visitlakegeorge.com
www.villageoflakegeorge.us
www.town.lakegeorge.ny.us

Material courtesy of Margaret Mannix, Town & Village of Lake George Historian

The Annual Lake George Antique Boat Rendezvous held in August. Margaret Mannix

97

LAKE LUZERNE

Lake Luzerne, a quaint small town in the southern part of Warren County, is west of Glens Falls and contains these hamlets: Lake Luzerne, Beartown, Danielstown, Fourth Lake, Hartman, and Lake Vanare. The Hudson River meets the Sacandaga River in the center of our town. Our population in the winter is approx. 3,347 but much larger in the summertime.

The Town of Lake Luzerne has been called the "Gateway to the Adirondacks." Tourists traveling north on Rt. 9N pass several lakes. The first four are natural: Luzerne, Second, Third, and Fourth. The state has a beautiful campsite at Fourth Lake. All the lakes flow into Lake Luzerne. In the 1920s Earl Woodward, the Dude Ranch Baron, bought a lot of land on both sides of 9N. Woodward built two lakes, Forest and Allure, while Lake Vanare was built by Van R. Rhodes.

The town was first settled after the French and Indian War. On August 14, 1767 Edward and Ebenezer Jessup and others received a grant for 4,100 acres from the King of England. The Jessup's home was on Main Street and now the site of the Adirondack Folk School. They lived here until the American Revolution and fled to Canada because they were Tories.

In 1792 our town received land from Queensbury and was named Fairfield. The name changed to Luzerne in 1808 after Chevalier de la Luzerne, a French nobleman who was sent to aid the Americans. In the 1950s the State Legislature changed the name to Lake Luzerne

Lumbering was the chief occupation of the area because of the vast forests. In 1835 there were 30 houses, sawmills, gristmills, and a distillery. In 1867 there was a large tannery on Wells Creek. The tannery expanded to a block long building and continued operating till 1920. The large chimney is still standing. There was also a pulp factory that later moved to a larger plant in Corinth.

Ketchum Tag factory began in 1922 and continues today on East Drive making metal ID tags, plastic ear tags, and tattoo equipment for animal identification.

In the late 1800s tourism became popular and hotels and boarding houses sprang up. The Wayside Inn housed two hundred guests, ten cottages, and had outdoor sports. Today on the hotel site is the Hadley-Luzerne Central School. Motels and guesthouses have replaced the original hotel structures.

Next came the Dude Ranch Era from the 1920 to 1992. Earl Woodward started with a farmhouse, then he built cottages, and started Northwood Dude Ranch. Later there were eight ranches in the Lake Vanare area of Lake Luzerne. The last ranch that he built from scratch was Hidden Valley, which now is the Double H, a camp for terminally-ill children.

Lake Luzerne had a number of childrens' camps: Camp Tekawitha, Marion Lodge, Pine Log Camp, and others but all but one have been abandoned. In 1980 Camp Tekawitha was bought by Toby Blumenthal, a concert pianist, and her husband Bert Phillips, a cellist from the Philadelphia Orchestra. Lake Luzerne Music Center is known worldwide.

POINTS OF INTEREST

Hadley-Luzerne Historical Society. Frances Kinnear Museum. 52 Main St., Lake Luzerne.

Lake Luzerne Heritage Day. Colonial-

98

DATE: _____ WEATHER: _____

MEMORIES: _____

_____

_____

_____

_____

_____

_____

_____

_____

_____

[Passport Stamp / Signature Here]

era educational demonstrations on the last Saturday in July.

Concerts in the Park. Thursdays at 7 pm. Park Pavilion, Lake Ave., Lake Luzerne.

Painted Pony Championship Rodeo. The oldest weekly rodeo in the U.S. Wednesdays, Fridays & Saturdays, July thru August. 703 Howe Rd., Lake Luzerne.

Adirondack Folk School. The only school in the country dedicated to teaching the arts, crafts, and culture of this unique Adirondack region. 51 Main St., Lake Luzerne.

Lynn Benevento Gallery. 4 Bridge St., Lake Luzerne.

Lake Luzerne Music Center. Concerts in July and August. 203 Lake Tour Rd., Lake Luzerne. www.luzernemusic.org

Mt. Kenyon Campground. 1571 Lake Ave., Lake Luzerne.

Harris Grocery and Camp Supplies. Rt. 9N by Fourth Lake, 887 Lake Ave., Lake Luzerne.

Rockwell Harmon House Visitor's Center, Chamber of Commerce. 37 Main St., Lake Luzerne.

Material courtesy of Bea Evens, Town of Lake Luzerne Historian

Painting of Ivy Island on Lake Luzerne. Lynn Benevento

99

PROVIDENCE

Providence is a town on the northwestern side of Saratoga County. It is a bordertown for the Great Sacandaga Lake and the Adirondack State Park with approx. 40 percent of its land being within the park boundaries. It also borders the Fulton County towns of Broadalbin and North Hampton. It contains these hamlets: Barkersville, Fayville, and Hagedorns Mills and these two lakes, Nancy and part of Desolation.

Prior to the start of the Revolutionary War, there were settlers living on land that is now Providence with the earliest known birth being Edward Shipman in 1766. At the onset of the War it is assumed that residents moved to more fortified areas for safety.

At the end of the Revolutionary War many veterans from New England moved to Providence with their families with most arriving around 1787. The town was named by the early residents after Providence, RI. The earliest known home that is still occupied was the home built on the South Line Road in 1789 by Pardon Davis from Dartmouth, Mass. Providence was established in 1796. It was carved out of what was then the Saratoga County Town of Galway and contained what is now the Town of Edinburgh.

As there are many streams in Providence, there was a thriving community living and working during the 1800s. There were many things manufactured but the most prominent was chairs by the Trevett family. Thousands of chairs were made from the mid-1800s to the early 1900s.

Today, Providence is the home to just over 1900 permanent residents and a number of summer residents and all enjoy the rural forested landscape and the Great Sacandaga Lake.

RECREATION

In addition to the Great Sacandaga Lake, Providence has three public campgrounds and a vast hiking trail network known as the Hennig Preserve which covers approx. 606 acres. It is open to the public for hiking and walking, cross-country skiing, snowshoeing, and nature study. 150 Centerline Road, Providence.

Directions to Hennig Preserve: Form Saratoga Springs take NY-29 west for 12.7 miles. Turn right onto Barkersville Rd/Co Rd 16 just before the bright yellow Waterwheel Village Country Store. Drive 2.4 miles and take a slight right at a 3-way corner to stay on Barkersville Rd. at the Providence Town Center. Continue on Barkersville for 0.5 miles. Take your second left onto Glenwild Rd. In 0.5 miles at stop sign take a right and stay on Glenwild Rd. Continue 0.75 miles and turn right on Centerline Road. Travel 0.5 miles to parking on right.

There are also many miles of abandoned town roads that wind their way through the forests of the town and are normally open for hiking.

Providence is mostly forested and many locals make a living harvesting the wood. Due to the hilly, rocky, sandy Adirondack soil, there is very little agriculture. Most residents are retired or working in one of the nearby cities of the Capital District and Mohawk Valley. We are friendly, close-knit, and welcome visitors!

Material courtesy of Ed Dandaraw, Town of Providence Historian

DATE: _____ WEATHER: _____

MEMORIES: _____

_____

_____

_____

_____

_____

_____

_____

_____

_____

_____

_____

_____

_____

_____

_____

[Passport Stamp / Signature Here]

The Hennig Preserve on Centerline Road in Providence. Ed Dandaraw

PUTNAM

Putnam is in the northernmost town in Washington County. It lies between Lake Champlain and Lake George. Putnam is about 7 miles long from north to south and comprises an area of 19,279 acres. It contains these hamlets: Putnam, Putnam Station, Glenburnie, and Wright.

In 1782 Joseph Haskins was the first settler. Then in 1784 William Hutton became the first permanent settler with his family and many families followed. Putnam was part of Westerfield (now Fort Ann) and became a separate town on Feb. 28, 1806. It was named in honor of General Israel Putnam, some of whose most remarkable military exploits were performed in this vicinity during the Revolutionary War.

The Town of Putnam was a farming community and the small industries that were initiated here were primarily for community service and needs. Today the community is rapidly changing to become one of New York's prime resort areas in Gull Bay and Glen Burnie on Lake George.

PLACES TO VISIT

Putnam District #1 School: Built in 1880 and was the fourth school on that site. It functioned as a school until 1928. It had many uses and was in danger of being torn down in the mid-1990s. The Putnam Seniors, a senior citizens' organization, saved the schoolhouse and restored it. Now, the school houses various historic materials and the Seniors continue to maintain the building as a museum. 365 Co. Rt. 2 in Putnam Station

Log Chapel: During the fall of 1933 most of the men of Putnam Station worked for 14 days constructing a church. The women helped by providing the food for the workers. The men used native trees to construct the 20 by 30-foot building, which later received an addition on the back. The congregation had its first service on Nov. 10, 1933 and church services have continued to the present. In addition to religious services, concerts are held in the chapel that is open to the public. 17163 Rt. 22, Putnam Station.

Material courtesy of Eileen Greely, Town of Putnam Historian

DATE: _____ WEATHER: _____

MEMORIES: _____

_____

_____

_____

_____

_____

_____

_____

_____

_____

_____

_____

_____

[Passport Stamp / Signature Here]

The Putnam Log Chapel on Rt. 22 in Putnam Station. Joan Rock

QUEENSBURY

The Town of Queensbury, located north of Glens Falls in Warren County, only has its northernmost part within the Blue Line of Adirondack Park. The town's location was important during the French and Indian War as the dividing line between the French and English land claims. The Great Military Road which traverses the town connected the Hudson River at Fort Edward (Washington County) with the shoreline of Lake George, roughly following Rt. 9 through Queensbury.

HISTORY

In the early 1760s, David Prindle of Connecticut received a large tract of land called the Queensbury Patent. Abraham Wing, a Quaker from Duchess County, purchased the patent from Prindle and is credited with bringing the first group of settlers to the area in 1763.

Growth in the town halted with the outbreak of the Revolutionary War. General Burgoyne's army passed through the town on the way to Saratoga. Following the Revolution, the area once again opened up to settlement. Just south of the Blue Line at Glens Falls, the shore of the Hudson River was alive with sawmills and factories that depended on the water power and lumber that moved down the river from the Adirondack forests.

Town growth began in earnest following World War II. Housing developments and small businesses grew up along Rt. 9, the north-south passageway between New York City and the Canadian border. Businesses and strip malls quickly provided employment and fulfilled the needs of consumers, which led to population growth.

POINTS OF INTEREST

SUNY Adirondack Community College. 640 Bay Rd., Queensbury.

Great Escape, a Six Flags amusement park. 89 Six Flags Dr., Queensbury.

Lower Adirondack Regional Arts Council (LARAC). Workshops, lectures, readings, and artists' demonstrations for children and adults. Holds an arts festival each June. 7 Lapham Pl., Glens Falls.

Adirondack Balloon Festival, held each fall at Floyd Bennett Memorial Airport. 443 Queensbury Ave., Queensbury.

'Taste of the North Country' is an annual food festival held between August and late September. www.glensfallstaste.com

At Blind Rock, a marker denotes a boulder which was known to Native Americans and early colonists as the landmark between lands held by the English and French prior to the French and Indian War (1754-63). It is the legendary scene of ambushes where soldiers were sometimes waylaid. It is located at the corner of Rt. 9 and Montray Rd.

World Awareness Children's Museum. 89 Warren St., Glens Falls.

The Hyde Collection is a museum that exhibits an important collection of European and American works of art and European antiques. Well worth visiting. 161 Warren St., Glens Falls.

Recreation opportunites abound including hiking, biking, and canoeing. Stretching from the Hudson River to Lake George a paved bicycle and walking trail passes through

DATE: _____ WEATHER: _____

MEMORIES: _____
_____
_____
_____
_____
_____
_____
_____
_____
_____
_____
_____
_____
_____
_____
_____

[Passport Stamp / Signature Here]

on the Hudson River, Glen Lake, and the historic Feeder Canal which connected the Hudson River with the Champlain Canal and markets north and south.

Material courtesy of Dr. Stan Cianfarano, Warren County Historical Society

Hundreds of balloonists gather at the Warren County Airport each Fall for the Annual Hot Air Balloon Festival that draws large crowds to the Town of Queensbury. Warren County Historical Society

105

STONY CREEK

The Town of Stony Creek is in the southwest corner of Warren County and the southeastern section of the Adirondack Park. It is approx. 15 miles west of Lake George and borders the towns of Thurman, Warrensburg, and Hadley. It is about 83 square miles. It includes the hamlets of Stony Creek, Harrisburg, and Knowelhurst.

HISTORY

The Town of Stony Creek was founded in 1852. It was in the original Town of Thurman, which was formed in 1792. In 1813, the same year that Warren County was formed, the town of Warrensburg split off and the area left was named Athol. At first the town was called Creek Center and then changed to Stony Creek. On November 3, 1852, the town of Athol was split into the towns of Stony Creek and Thurman.

The population in 1855 was 913; the permanent population in 2010 was 767. Lumbering and allied industries were the main source of income in the early days including a peg factory, broom handle factory, tannery, woodenware factory, and cooper's shop. Many residents farmed for their own sustenance. At one time there were five churches, three post offices, and a general store. There are 18 cemeteries located around town.

INTERESTING PLACES TO VISIT

There is an information lean-to located at the four corners in the center of town. It is where you will find a locator map of the town, along with brochures of town businesses and places of interest. A free map of the area is available for a self-guided driving tour. This map will also help in locating trailheads, boat launches, local cemeteries, historical markers, businesses, and special events.

Stony Creek Chamber of Commerce. www.stonycreekny.com

Stony Creek Free Library. 37 Harrisburg Rd., Stony Creek. stonycreekfreelibrary.sals.edu

Historic Sites to Visit:
Dean Homestead and Museum. Local history and artifacts, 4 Murray Rd., Stony Creek, call for hours. 518-696-5211

Stony Creek Historical Association Museum. Corner of Murray Rd. and Lanfear Rd.

Special Events:
Stony Creek Mountain Days Festival held on the first full weekend in August.

Music in the Park held every Tuesday night in July and August. Both of these events are held at the John O'Neil Green Meadow Park and Beach. The park has a basketball court, softball field, and playgrounds.

Restaurants/Lodging:
Stony Creek Inn. www.stonycreekinn.net

1,000 Acres. Dude Ranch Resort, trail rides, swimming, sports, etc. 465 Warrensburg Rd., Stony Creek. www.1000acres.com

Camping:
Thomas Creek Campground. 360 Hadley Rd., Stony Creek 518-696-2354

Stony Creek Family Campground. 18 Grist Mill Rd., Stony Creek. www.stonycreekcampground.com

Places to Hike:
Wilcox Wild Forest, Dean Farm Trail, Arrow Trail, West Stony Creek, and other State Land.

DATE: _____ WEATHER: _____

MEMORIES: _____

_____

_____

_____

_____

_____

_____

_____

_____

_____

_____

_____

_____

_____

_____

[Passport Stamp / Signature Here]

Places to Canoe/Kayak:
Lens Lake, Harrisburg Lake, Wilcox Lake, Brownell Lake and Willis Lake.

Places to Fish:
Stony Creek, Roaring Branch, Harrisburg Lake, Lens Lake, Wilcox Lake, Brownell Lake, and Willis Lake.

Material courtesy of Cynthia Cameron, Town of Stony Creek Historian

Harrisburg in the Town of Stony Creek. Cynthia Cameron

THURMAN

Thurman lies in the western part of Warren County, Southern Adirondacks. It is bounded on the east by the Hudson River, across from Warrensburg, and neighbored by the towns of Johnsburg, Stony Creek, and Wells.

HISTORY

At its founding by John Thurman in 1792, the town encompassed 800 sq. mi., and included all of that land that is now Warren County except for the towns of Lake Luzerne and Queensbury. Vigorous marketing created growth until 1798, when new towns began breaking away, eventually paring Thurman to 93.8 sq. mi. It was home to farmers, loggers, and a smattering of innkeepers, shopkeepers, preachers, and teachers. Some clustered in little hamlets: Athol, Thurman Station, High Street, The Glen, and Kenyontown.

In 1872 Dr. Thomas Durant built Thurman Station and the railroad tracks through Thurman. His Adirondack Branch gave way to the D&H, then CP Rail, carrying goods, tradesmen, and tourists. The station was demolished in 1933, and service was discontinued 1983, to be restored after Warren County bought the tracks in the 1990s and contracted with operators. A new station stands where the old one was demolished in the 1930s.

Today agriculture still thrives in Thurman. Warren County's four largest commercial maple sugar operations lie within the township, which also is home to a goat and sheep farm that produces nationally-acclaimed cheeses. There are tree farms and sawmills and a vegetable and poultry operation. Visitors are welcomed for tours, demonstrations, samples, and shopping at various events during the year.

SEASONAL ACTIVITIES

March:
Thurman Maple Days
Tours, talks, demonstrations and food.
www.thurmanmapledays.com

Thurman Maple Sugar Party
Buffet, live music, and jack wax (maple syrup poured over fresh snow).
www.thurmanmaplesugarparty.com

October:
Thurman Fall Farm Tour
Animals, hayrides, farm bounty, and food.
www.thurmanfallfarmtour.com

July:
Thurman Showcase
Expo of businesses, artisans, and organizations around Thurman Station.
www.thurmanshowcase.com

Nettle Meadow has goats, sheep & llamas, and cheese shopping. www.nettlemeadow.com

Martin's Lumber offers woods walks, sawmill demos, and shopping. Contact them at www.martins-lumber.com

Whitefield's Farm raises cage-free chickens and turkeys, and sells a large variety of vegetables. Spicy Salad mix is a local favorite. They can be contacted on Facebook.

For information regarding all Thurman events, visit www.thurmannyevents.com.

But visit anytime! Fish, boat or swim in the Hudson River and Garnet Lake. Climb Crane Mountain, which can be accessed from the Thurman trailhead.

Like boating? Stay at The Glen Lodge B&B

DATE: _____ WEATHER: _____

MEMORIES: _____

_____

_____

_____

_____

_____

_____

_____

_____

_____

_____

_____

_____

[Passport Stamp / Signature Here]

and plan rafting, canoeing, kayaking or tubing. There are also miles of snowmobile trails or ski nearby Gore. www.theglengodge.com

Daggett Lake is a private lake that offers tents, RVs, and cabins for your family. www.daggettlake.com

Whitewater rafting trips for the family: www.wildwaters.net

For canoe, kayak, tube rentals, guided trips, fishing gear: www.beaverbrook.net

Snowmobiling: www.thurmanconnection.com

You'll find an old-fashioned warm welcome in Thurman, a town that cultivates its heritage.

Material courtesy of Persis "Perky" Granger, Writer & Resident

The Town of Thurman has four large commercial maple sugar operations and during March "Thurman Maple Days" are celebrated with talks, demonstrations, and food. Perky Granger

109

WARRENSBURG

The Town of Warrensburg is in central Warren County and in the southeastern Adirondacks. It is located on Rt. 9, northwest of I-87 (Adirondack Northway) Exit 23.

Following the Revolutionary War, homesteaders from the lower Hudson Valley and Connecticut moved to the area now known as Warrensburg - the earliest recorded being Andrew and Ruth Vowers with four children, settling along the Schroon River in 1783. Numerous families arrived in the area now comprising Warrensburg and Thurman. In 1813 the Town of Thurman was divided into the Town of Warrensburgh, situated on the east side of the Hudson River, and the Town of Athol (later renamed Thurman), on the West side. The Schroon River, forming part of Warrensburgh's eastern border, drops 70 feet in three miles. Three dams built here provided water for tanneries and power for sawmills, gristmills, and electric generation.

The area's vast pine and hemlock forests provided the first industries - lumbering, potash-making, and leather tanning. Notable developers were Woodward, Bishop, Warren, Osborn and Burhans. Albert C. Emerson married into the Woodward family, and became a major business developer and banker. His sons, Louis and James developed shirt, pants, and pulp and paper, capitalizing on the abundant water power available.

By the turn of the 20th Century tourism developed, and the town boasted of four major hotels and numerous rooming and boarding houses. With the aforementioned industries declining steeply in the latter half of the 1900s, recreation ascended and the mountains, lakes, and rivers provide the major industry today.

PLACES TO VISIT

Warrensburg contains more than 400 buildings listed on both NYS and National Historic Registers. Beautiful homes gracing its tree-lined streets and remains of its once thriving industries provide interesting documented walking tours in any season.

Warrensburgh Museum of Local History. History through photos and artifacts, arranged chronologically, from geological times to present. 3754 Main St.

Historic Mills District. Remnants of a thriving industrial town - tanning, sawmills, and lumber yards, shirt factory, sash & blind planing mill, shoe peg factory, woolen mill, and pants factory and electric generating plants. River St. (Rt. 418) between Osborne and Milton Ave. bridges.

Farmers' Market Park. Located on River Street, at site of woolen mill dam and planing mill. Open Friday afternoons.

Warrensburg Fish Hatchery. Self-guided tours of breeding facilities, brook and rainbow trout, as well as Atlantic salmon. A picnic area with canoe access to the Hudson River, pavilions and grills, restrooms, playground, and sports facilities for basketball, softball, volleyball and horseshoes. Open 8 am – 4 pm. 145 Fish Hatchery Rd. 518-623-2877

Hackensack Mountain Park & Recreation Area. Small Adirondack mountain located in the hamlet and rising approx. 1,357 feet has a network of trails to top, and great views of Warrensburg and Three Sisters Mountains to the west. Easy access on Prospect St. or Warren St. www.upyondafarm.com/hackensack.html

DATE: _____ WEATHER: _____

MEMORIES: _____

_____

_____

_____

_____

_____

_____

_____

_____

_____

[Passport Stamp / Signature Here]

Warren County Nature & Cross-Country Ski Trails. Free parking, access to trails, and interesting riverside rock formations. During the winter season, Cronin's Gold Course permits cross-country skiing on its fairways. Located along the Hudson River on Golf Course Rd. (upper Hudson Street).

Pack Demonstration Forest. Pack A DEC-operated summer camp that offers 2,500 acres of forest lands, including a lake and trails leading to mountain vistas. Visit the Giant Grandmother's Tree, too. Named for Charles Lathrop Pack, it was donated to Syracuse University and is now operated by NYS DEC. Off Rt. 9, at 276 Pack Forest Rd. N of the Warrensburg.

Morry Stein Park & Beach at Echo Lake. Offers a beach staffed by lifeguards during the summer, a pavilion, picnic tables, playground equipment, and basketball net. Entrance off Hudson St. (adjacent to cemetery).

Material courtesy of Steve Parisi, Director of Warrensburgh Museum of Local History

Floyd Bennett Park Bandstand on Rt. 28 and US Highway 9 in Warrensburg. Warrensburgh Historical Society

111

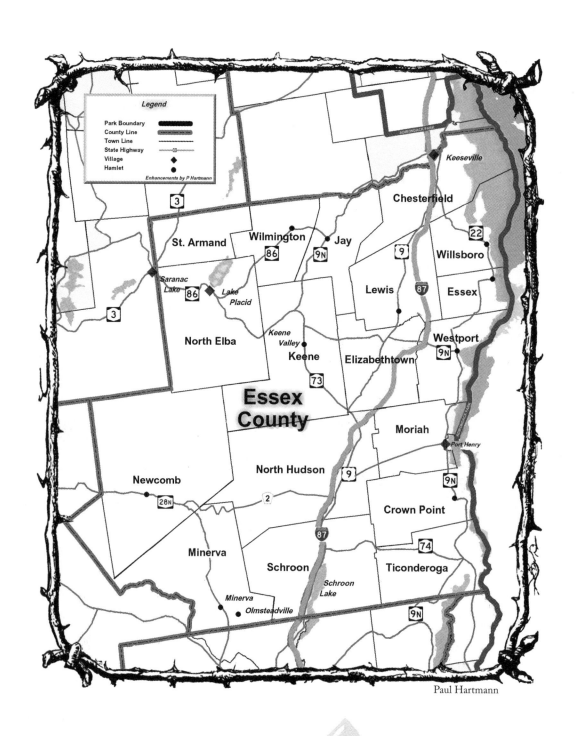

Legend

Park Boundary
County Line
Town Line
State Highway
Village
Hamlet

Enhancements by P Hartmann

Paul Hartmann

Essex County

Keeseville, Chesterfield, Wilmington, Jay, Willsboro, St. Armand, Lewis, Essex, Saranac Lake, Lake Placid, Keene Valley, Westport, North Elba, Keene, Elizabethtown, Moriah, Port Henry, North Hudson, Newcomb, Crown Point, Minerva, Schroon, Ticonderoga, Schroon Lake, Olmsteadville

CHAPTER 4

REGION IV:
ESSEX COUNTY

CHESTERFIELD

The Town of Chesterfield is in northeastern Essex County 15 miles south of Plattsburgh. It is located between Lake Champlain and the Amusable River and includes part of the Village of Keeseville, and the hamlets of Port Douglas and Port Kent.

Chesterfield was founded in 1802. The population was made up of farmers, loggers, and a few iron ore miners.

The Village was settled in 1808 and originally called Anderson Falls. Around 1812 the name was changed to Keeseville, after a local manufacturer and businessman. The early village was an industrial area devoted, in part, to lumber, iron processing, and milling.

From 1850 to the early 1900s the Ausable Horse Nail Co. "Complex" revolutionized the production of iron nails. It was here that a local blacksmith invented a horse nail machine that produced 200 lbs. of nails in the amount of time previously needed to make 10 lbs. by hand. R. Prescott and Sons took over the "Complex" and was a manufacturer of wood products in the early 1900s. In 1960 the factory closed and the "Complex" became vacant.

In January 2013, voters decided in a referendum to end the fabled history of the village by dissolving it outright. By the end of 2014 the Village Keeseville became part of the two bordering towns of AuSable and Chesterfield.

PLACES TO VISIT

Ausable Chasm. Descend hundreds of feet and walk on natural stone walkways and gaze upon eons of geologic history etched in stone. Open year-round. 2144 Rt. 9, Keeseville.

North Country Underground Railroad Museum. Poignant exhibits portray compelling stories of fugitives from slavery who passed through Northeastern New York and the Champlain Valley on their way to Quebec and Ontario, Canada. 1131 Mace Chasm Road, Keeseville.

Heritage House Museum. Located in the Town of Chesterfield's Heritage Center. Open 7 days a week, 9 am – 4 pm, from the first Saturday in May to the last Saturday in October. 96 Clinton Street, Keeseville. 518-834-5280

Adirondack Architectural Heritage (AARCH) preserves the architecture and communities of the Adirondacks through education, action, and advocacy. 1790 Main St., Keeseville. www.aarch.org

Places to Hike & Canoe:
Poke-O-Moonshine Mountain. Trailhead on Rt. 9 in Keeseville.

Ausable River or Lake Champlain.

Lake Transportation:
Lake Champlain Ferry Transportation runs June thru October, Vermont to New York.

New York State Boat Launch Site on Schuyler Road in the Town of Chesterfield.

Material courtesy of Shelly Davis, Town of Chesterfield Assessor

DATE: _____ WEATHER: _____

MEMORIES: _____

_____

_____

_____

_____

_____

_____

_____

_____

_____

_____

_____

_____

_____

_____

_____

_____

[Passport Stamp / Signature Here]

The poignant exhibits at the The North Star Underground Railroad Museum portray compelling stories of fugitives from slavery who passed through northeastern New York and the Champlain Valley on their way to Quebec and Ontario, Canada. The museum is located in the Town of Chesterfield Heritage Center at 1131 Mace Chasm Road in Keeseville. North Country Underground Railroad Museum

CROWN POINT

The Town of Crown Point is located in eastern Essex County. It is bordered on the east by Lake Champlain, on the north by Moriah, and on the south by Ticonderoga. It includes the following hamlets and lake: Burdick Crossing, Crown Point, Cold Spring Park, Crown Point Center, Factoryville, Ironville, and Eagle Lake.

HISTORY

The boundaries of Crown Point contain histories that pertain to French and English exploration/development/control and their interaction with Native Americans. The fact that whoever controlled the lake at Crown Point also controlled the southern part of the lake was a major factor both in the French and Indian War and the Revolutionary War. Today, the state-maintained ruins of French and English forts stand in tribute to this time. At this same location stands the second Lake Champlain Bridge along with a lighthouse and a statue of Samuel de Champlain created by French artist Auguste Rodin. The bridge, lighthouse, forts, a museum, and a large campsite are all within the confines of a New York State Park.

Crown Point history also revolves around the discovery of a hi-grade vein of iron ore. The first stone furnace was located several miles from the lake. Soon after, many large furnaces started to pop up along the lake (mainly at the location presently known as Monitor Bay). Subsequently, a railroad was built to transport iron ore from the mountains directly to Monitor Bay. 'Monitor Bay' received its name from the a Civil War armored battleship whose iron plate was made from the iron ore of the Crown Point mountains.

POINTS OF INTEREST

Crown Point has a marina that will accommodate 20 boats and provides water, electricity, a restroom, and showers. Town offices and a campsite are also located at Monitor Bay.

At the Crown Point State Historic Site, visitors can explore the ruins of the original 18th Century structures and tour the newly renovated museum which includes an auditorium where visitors can watch an award-winning multimedia orientation program before touring the exhibits and grounds. Across the street, the historic Crown Point Pier and Champlain Memorial Lighthouse, also beautifully restored in 2009, are open to the public. 21 Grandview Dr., Crown Point.

Penfield Museum exhibits the Civil War, the birth of the electrical age, the mining and processing of iron ore along with displays of early Adirondack life. 703 Creek Rd., Crown Point. 518-597-3804

Crown Point also boasts a modern fish hatchery that supplies fish throughout the Adirondacks. Gunnison's Orchard, one of the oldest establishments in the Adirondacks is located along Lake Champlain. There are two convenience stores, several summer snack bar/restaurants, two bed and breakfasts. The town also has several contractors and master carpenters.

The Town of Crown Point is dotted with many small farms. There is one farm that produces certified organic milk.

Crown Point has four bodies of water that can be accessed by car. But, there are also several small lakes and ponds to explore that can only

DATE: _____ WEATHER: _____

MEMORIES: _____

_____

_____

_____

_____

_____

_____

_____

_____

_____

_____

_____

_____

_____

[Passport Stamp / Signature Here]

be accessed by trail.

There are historic sites at the juncture of the Crown Point Bridge which spans Lake Champlain. This bridge is a half-mile span that also contains a secure sidewalk and a bike path. There is a historical district located in the center of town with original buildings that date back to the early 1800s that are along a large central park.

Please visit the town of Crown Point's website, www.townofcrownpoint.com.

Material courtesy of Charles Harrington, Town Supervisor

The historic remains of the British fort at Crown Point. Kimberly Woods

117

ELIZABETHTOWN

Elizabethtown, the Essex County seat, is known as the Gateway to the Adirondack High Peaks. It is approx. 22 miles southeast of Lake Placid and 10 miles northwest of Westport. The town the hamlets of Elizabethtown and New Russia, the Black River and the Bouquet River, and two small lakes, Lincoln Pond and New Pond.

Revolutionary War veterans from Vermont first settled Elizabethtown in 1792. At that time the Upper Boquet River valley was known as Pleasant Valley. The town was formally organized on February 12, 1798 and included an area of 822 square miles. The town and the village at its center were named after two women named Elizabeth Gilliland. They were the wife and a daughter of landholder William Gilliland, who came to Essex County before the Revolutionary War.

During the early years, lumber and maple sugaring were important industries. Tourism eventually replaced lumber as the main industry in the late 1800s.

Quaint, in a laid-back and charming way, our little town is peaceful and quiet, with friendly people, offering museums, historic homes, a hospital, restaurants, grocery, library, shops, farmer's market, B&B's, motels, flower shop, hardware, drug and convenience stores, tennis courts, hiking trails, fishing, bicycling, snowshoeing, cross-country skiing, and a breathtaking 9-hole golf course. It's the perfect spot for outdoor enthusiasts of all pursuits. We are a year-round destination.

INTERESTING PLACES TO VISIT

Adirondack History Center Museum, displays artifacts from over two centuries of life in Essex County and the central Adirondacks. Also contains Brewster Library for research and there is a 58' fire tower to climb. Open seasonally from late May thru mid-October, 10 am – 5 pm, 7 days a week. 7590 Court St. Elizabethtown. www.adkhistorycenter.org

Cobble Hill Golf Course, Court St., Rt. 9, Elizabethtown. www.etownny.com

Hurricane Mt. fire tower, the 35' tower was built in 1919 on the 3,694' summit but was closed in 1979. The tower will be restored for interpretive and educational purposes. Directions: From Elizabethtown go 6.8 miles west from the junction of Rts. 9 and 9N. The trailhead is opposite the parking lot on the north side of Rt. 9N. Follow the red trail markers for 2.6 miles to the tower. The view is great even without climbing the tower.

Lincoln Pond State Campground, swimming, boating, fishing, and 35 campsites. 4363 Lincoln Pond Rd., Elizabethtown. From (I-87), Exit 31 west to Elizabethtown, turn left on Co. Rt. 7 & travel 6 miles.

Elizabethtown Library. 8256 River St. www.cefls.org/elizabethtown.html

Historic Hand-Hale District. Two adjoining properties located on both sides of Rt. 9N (River St.).

Blueberry Trails Map. 30 different trails for hiking, snowshoeing, mountain biking, horseback riding, skiing, and snowmobiling in Elizabethtown. Directions: from the intersections of Rts. 9N & 9 in Elizabethtown go west on 9N to Lord Rd. on the right. Follow Lord Rd. for about 0.1 miles, the trailhead and parking are on the left.

DATE: _____ WEATHER: _____

MEMORIES: _____

_____

_____

_____

_____

_____

_____

_____

_____

_____

_____

_____

_____

_____

[Passport Stamp / Signature Here]

Elizabethtown Social Center. Offers classes in fitness and art, sponsors community events and has space available for rent. 626 Rt. 9. www.elizabethtownsocialcenter.org

Adirondack Outdoor Company. Trapping supplies, taxidermy, and other outdoor-related supplies and gear. 8549 Rt. 9, Lewis (4 miles N of Elizabethtown). www.adirondackoutdoor.com

Champlain Area Trails. Site with hiking trail maps. www.champlainareatrails.com

Material courtesy of Mary McGowan, Elizabethtown-Lewis Chamber of Commerce

Cobble Hill Golf Course is one of the oldest in America. Built in 1896 it offers nine challenging holes among tall pines and spectacular mountain views. Margaret Bartley

119

ESSEX

Cradled between the Adirondack Mountains and Lake Champlain, Essex is a town of unlimited potential waiting to be discovered by visitors, businesses, and residents alike.

Essex has spectacular views of the Adirondacks, Lake Champlain and the Green Mountains of Vermont that change with the seasons. Rich farmlands and forests surround the five hamlets: Boquet, Brookfield, Essex, Whallons Bay, and Whallonsburgh. It is 26 miles south of Plattsburgh.

The region was first settled around 1765 with the intention of forming a baronial estate like those of the lower Hudson River for landowner and investor, William Gilliland. Essex was formed from its neighboring town, Willsborough in 1805 and was an important shipbuilding community at the time. The current population is 671 according to the 2010 census. And being a summer vacation destination its population increases significantly during the summer months.

The lakeside hamlet of Essex is on the National Register of Historical Sites and offers a unique combination of historic architecture and outdoors activities. There are various lodging and dining establishments, marinas, specialty shops, art, health and fitness studios, and a lovely public park on Lake Champlain to enjoy. All is within walking distance after a short ferry boat ride from Charlotte, Vermont.

RECREATION

The Lake Champlain Paddlers Trail has two stops on the Essex shoreline for picnicking and day hiking. And there are over 75 miles of hiking trails in the area, 24 miles of which are within the town of Essex. For trail information:

www.champlainareatrails.com

Saturday Morning Bikers meet at Essex Deli at 7:30 am sharp. Bicycle 20-30 picturesque miles. Stops at local eateries and end back at the deli or at your choice of destination.

Scenic Byway (Lakes to Locks Passage). www.bikethebyways.org

Lake Champlain Committee Paddle Trails provides safe places on the lake to canoe or kayak. It includes 40 locations on NY and VT public and private lands, providing access to more than 600 lakeshore and island campsites. www.lakechamplaincommittee.org/explore

POINTS OF INTEREST

Essex is home to many local farms which serve Essex residents, neighboring communities and passersby with an incredible selection of organic produce, dairy, meat, legumes, and various items. Find a list of farms at www.essexnewyork.com/farms-parks/

Nationally recognized author Kristin Kimball wrote "The Dirty Life" about her first years of farming in Essex. Essex Farm tours are a wonderful experience for those who like to stumble upon farm stand booths. 2503 Rt. 22, a mile from the Essex/Charlotte ferry. www.kristinkimball.com/events

Lake Champlain Transportation Company. Ferry transportation between Essex and Charlotte, Vermont.

Adirondack Art Association. Gallery featuring Adirondack artists, 2752 Essex Rd., Essex. www.adirondackartassociation.com

Neighborhood Nest. Art, antiques, nature, Main St., Essex.

DATE: _____ WEATHER: _____

MEMORIES: _____

_____

_____

_____

_____

_____

_____

_____

_____

_____

_____

_____

_____

_____

_____

[Passport Stamp / Signature Here]

Cupola House Gallery & Emporium. Artists, antiques, quilts & collectibles, 2278 Main St., Essex.

Beggs Point Park. Playground, fishing pier, boat launch, site of horseshoe nail & window sash factories.

Visit www.essexnewyork.com for information on lodging, dining, shopping, docking, hiking, local government and other interests.

Material courtesy of Olive Alexander & Sharon Boisen, Essex Residents

A July 4th parade with a float celebrating farming in the Town of Essex. Essex is home to many local farms with an incredible selection of organic produce, dairy, meat, legumes, and various items. Sharon Boisen

121

JAY

The Town of Jay covers 68.3 square miles in NE Essex Co. It is located where the East and West Branches of the Ausable River meet in AuSable Forks to form one confluence. The town consists of three hamlets: Au Sable Forks, Jay, and Upper Jay.

HISTORY

The Town of Jay was originally known of as "Mallory's Bush" after it was founded by Nathaniel Mallory, its first settler (c. 1797). In 1798 the town separated from Willsboro to become its own entity, and was named in honor of New York State Governor John Jay.

INTERESTING PLACES TO VISIT

Town of Jay Museum & Genealogy Center. Unique historical photo collection. 11 School Lane, Au Sable Forks.

Tahawus Lodge. Dance Studio and Gallery & Tea Time Antique Gallery. Main St., Au Sable Forks.

Jay Entertainment & Music Center. Concerts and dance recitals. Parkside Drive, Jay.

Jay Craft Center. Pottery and local crafts. Rt. 9, Jay.

Burdick/Young Gallery. Pottery, jewelry and prints. Rt. 86, Jay.

Adirondack Life Magazine. Rt. 9, Jay.

The Hollywood Theatre. Movies and matinees. Main St., Au Sable Forks.

The Alpaca Shoppe. Alpaca fiber products. Rt. 9, Jay.

On Saturdays during the summer there are concerts on the Village Green, which is located at the corner of Parkside Dr. and Rt. 9, Jay.

Au Sable Forks Free Library. Church Lane, Au Sable Forks.

Historic Sites:
Covered Bridge. John Fountain Rd., Jay.

Recovery Lounge. Building is a Member of NYS Historical Registry. It was the first local Ford Dealer owned by Keith & Branch Co. Rt. 9, Upper Jay.

Wells Memorial Library is also a member of the NYS Historical Registry. Rt. 9, Upper Jay.

Asgaard Farm is the former home of world renowned artist Rockwell Kent. The farm is in full operation with free-range cattle, pigs, chickens, and goats. Tours and farm products available. Sheldrake Rd., Au Sable Forks. www.asgaardfarm.com

Places to Hike, Canoe, Fish:
Trailhead to Jay Mountain, access on Jay Mountain Rd.

Ausable River, premier east coast fishing destination.

Material courtesy of Randall Douglas, Supervisor & Carol A. Greenley-Hackel, Deputy Town Clerk

DATE: _____ WEATHER: _____

MEMORIES: _____

_____

_____

_____

_____

_____

_____

_____

_____

_____

_____

_____

_____

_____

_____

_____

_____

[Passport Stamp / Signature Here]

The Jay Covered Bridge on John Fountain Rd. Carol A. Greenley-Hackel

123

KEENE

The Town of Keene is in Essex County and consists of the hamlets of Keene, Keene Valley, and St. Huberts. It is called "Home of the High Peaks" because within its boundaries are the summits of 26 of the 46 High Peaks of the Adirondacks, an enduring attraction for both those who climb them and those who just look at them.

The first settlers arrived in the 1790s. Many subsequent arrivals were from New Hampshire, and the town took its name from Keene, New Hampshire. In 1808 Keene was formed as a separate town. Most early residents were farmers, but iron ore deposits near the hamlet of Keene were exploited until the early 1900s. Forges, sawmills, and grist mills used the abundant water power of the East Branch of the Ausable River.

In the 1850s, a few pioneering artists made their way to Keene Valley and engaged local residents to guide them to scenic locations such as the Upper Ausable Lake. Keene Valley's most famous guide, Orson "Old Mountain" Phelps, even guided one to the summit of Mount Marcy, with Phelps later cutting the first crude trail up Marcy in 1861. After the Civil War, more artists arrived, followed by other visitors who wanted to see the grand scenery for themselves.

By 1900, three large hotels and many smaller lodging establishments were doing a brisk summer business. Many visitors later built second homes, keeping the local sawmills and tradesmen busy into the 1920s. The construction of paved roads ended the need for as many farms or other local production, and the population shrank from 1,600 to around 600 before slowly rebounding to just over 1,000 at present.

The mountains remain Keene's major attraction. Hikers, rock and ice climbers, and skiers visit on a regular basis. Scenic hikes can be as short as the quarter-mile flat jaunt to the base of Roaring Brook Falls in St. Huberts or as challenging as the 25-mile 9,000-foot vertical traverse of Mount Marcy and the Great Range. A perfect "starter" climb is Rooster Comb Mt., accessed by a 2.5 mile trail that starts just south of Keene Valley. The trailhead for Rooster Comb is on the right 0.4 mi. past the High Peaks sign in the center of Keene Valley.

Skiers can explore the Jackrabbit Ski Trail that leads to Lake Placid and beyond while the cliffs in Chapel Pond Pass attract technical climbers in all seasons. Photographers will find many scenic locations along the valley and at the Cascade Lakes on Rt. 73 heading toward Lake Placid.

Businesses include several bed & breakfasts, restaurants, delis, and diners, including the Noonmark Diner in Keene Valley (1770 Rt. 73 Scenic, Keene Valley) where one can see an historic photo of one of the truly grand hotels. The Mountaineer store in Keene Valley (1866 Rt. 73 Scenic) provides gear and advice for both climbers and fishermen, and several guide services continue that honored Keene Valley tradition.

While in Keene Valley visit their beautiful old library constructed in 1896 at 1796 Rt. 73 Scenic. Also stop by the quaint library in Keene, Scenic Rt. 73.

Material courtesy of Tony Goodwin, Keene Valley Resident and Author

DATE: _____ WEATHER: _____

MEMORIES: _____

_____

_____

_____

_____

_____

_____

_____

_____

_____

_____

_____

_____

_____

_____

_____

[Passport Stamp / Signature Here]

The Noonmark Diner (1770 Rt. 73 Scenic, in Keene Valley) is a favorite
restaurant for hikers, tourist, and local residents. Tony Goodwin

LAKE PLACID VILLAGE

Lake Placid is a quaint village located within the Town of North Elba nestled in the beautiful Adirondacks. Lake Placid was incorporated in 1900 with a population of 3,000 friendly people. First settlers arrived in the early 1800s and were mostly farmers. In 1900 with the development of the Lake Placid Club, the village became a tourist and sports center, which eventually lead to the village becoming the home of the 1932 and 1980 Winter Olympics.

To those who thrive on Adirondack outdoor adventure, the list of options is infinite. Endless miles of challenging backcountry trails are perfect for hiking and mountain biking. The sparkling lakes, rivers and ponds are perfect for canoeing and kayaking, while the nearby West Branch of the Ausable River is a fly fisherman's dream. Licensed Adirondack guides are available for fishing, hunting, and other backcountry pursuits. At any time of year, a world of outdoor opportunities awaits in the Adirondacks.

Golfers find it difficult to keep their heads down as some of the most breathtaking views of the mountains and lakes can be enjoyed from the cedar-lined fairways and rolling greens of the area's signature and historic golf courses, some over 100 years old.

Biking is also popular with extreme downhill trails, quiet country roads, or Ironman training runs, so this region is a must-ride destination for both the knobby and road-tire sets. From Lake Placid, road cyclists can try out the Ironman loop.

Anglers are lured to cast a line into the famed West Branch of the Ausable River, the longtime fly-fisherman's paradise that is nationally recognized for its six miles of designated catch-and-release fishing. Lake Placid itself is known for its abundant rainbow and lake trout.

Lake Placid continues to host contemporary world class competitions year-round, including popular races such as the Lake Placid marathon and Ironman USA in summer. The calendar is brimming with events, and from the traditional 4th of July celebrations to LaCross tournaments to weekly Sinfonietta concerts in the park, there is something to add to every day's itinerary.

Of course, if you haven't run out of time yet, there's always window shopping on Lake Placid's Main Street, with treasures by Adirondack artisans, antiques, outdoor gear and designer clothing. www.lakeplacid.com

POINTS OF INTEREST

Lake Placid Olympic Center & Museum. The center is the ice skating rink where the men defeated the Russians in the 1980 Olympics and where they won the gold medal. The museum has displays of Lake Placid's rich sports history from 1895 to the present including the 1932 & 1980 Olympic Winter Games. 2634 Main St.

Lake Placid Center of Arts. Intimate 350-seat theatre gives you the opportunity to see your favorite artists, (music, theater, and dance) in an intimate space. 7 Algonquin Dr.

Palace Theater. 2430 Main St.

Lake Placid Railroad Station. Museum and home of the Adirondack Scenic Railroad that runs round trip passenger trains to Saranac Lake. www.adirondackrr.com/lakeplacid.html

DATE: _____ WEATHER: _____

MEMORIES: _____

_____

_____

_____

_____

_____

_____

_____

_____

_____

_____

_____

_____

[Passport Stamp / Signature Here]

Placid and Mirror Lakes. Swimming, canoeing, kayaking, and water skiing.

Whiteface Club & Resort Golf Course. 373 Whiteface Inn Ln. www.whitefaceclubresort.com

Crowne Plaza Resort & Golf Club. 101 Olympic Dr. www.lakeplacidcp.com

Lake Placid Club Mountain Course. 88 Morningside Dr. www.lakeplacidresort.com

Material courtesy of Beverly Reid, Lake Placid Historian & Kimberly Rielly, Director of Communications, Lake Placid Convention and Visitors Bureau/Regional Office of Sustainable Tourism

A view of Lake Placid from the air. The Olympic Center is in the bottom left (white building next to the high school) and the village and stores are along the shore of Lake Placid with Whiteface Mt. in the upper right. Regional Office of Sustainable Tourism

LEWIS

The Town of Lewis is located in the northeastern section of Essex County in the eastern Adirondack Mountains. It is 84 sq. mi. in area with a population of 1382. Its highest point is Jay Mt., 3,600 feet.

It was settled in 1796 and incorporated in 1805. It was named in honor of then Governor of New York, Morgan Lewis, a soldier, jurist, and politician. The town sits between Lake Champlain to the east and the Jay Mountain Range to the west. Abundant waterways fueled the mills and forges that were established by a growing population in the early 1800s. With two rich iron ore veins located in Lewis the iron industry proliferated with concomitant businesses being established.

As the population of Lewis grew in the early 1800s, the signs of an established community such as schools and churches appeared. Cyrus Comstock, father of Congregationalism, was sent to Lewis to spread God's word. He established the first Congregational Church in Essex County, which was erected in Lewis. Father Comstock was also the inventor of the Comstock Wagon. Lewis continued to see growth throughout the 19th Century with small enterprises such as hotels, general stores, distilleries, forges, tanneries, and a library. With the coming of the 20th Century, the small enterprises begin to disappear and the population saw a decline resulting from the depletion of iron ore in the town.

Lewis received national attention through the women's suffrage activities of Inez Milholland in the early 20th Century. Inez was one of the first woman attorneys in New York and was active in both the labor and voting rights movement. She will always be remembered riding a white horse leading a parade to support the right of women to vote on the day before the inauguration of President Woodrow Wilson in 1913. Her comment, "Mr. President, how long must women wait for liberty," helped to galvanize the movement. Inez died in 1916 before the passage of the 20th Amendment.

With the Northway, Interstate 87, opening in 1967, the north/south traffic no longer used Rt. 9 and many of the restaurants, motels, and stores closed. This was the impetus for Lewis to become the bedroom community it is today. Lewis has the renowned International Meadowmount School of Music, and NYCO Minerals, which mines Wollastonite, a mineral used in plastics and paint. Lewis also is the site for the Essex County Public Safety building and jail. During the Cold War, Lewis was also the site of one of the Atlas missile silos.

The 2010 census revealed that Lewis was one of the fastest growing towns in Essex County.

PLACES TO VISIT

Father Comstock & Inez Milholland gravesites. Both located west of the First Congregational Church of Lewis on Rt. 9.

Meadowmount School of Music. Classical concerts each Sunday during the summer. 1424 Co. Rt. 10, Westport.

Trailhead to Poke-o-Moonshine Mountain fire tower. Starts at the state campsite off Rt. 9, south of Keeseville.

First Congregational Church of Lewis. On the National Register of Historic Places. Rt. 9 in Lewis, north of the post office.

Community Gardens near the First Congregational Church of Lewis on Rt. 9.

DATE: _____ WEATHER: _____

MEMORIES: _____

_____

_____

_____

_____

_____

_____

_____

_____

_____

_____

_____

_____

_____

[Passport Stamp / Signature Here]

Milholland Park. A day-use picnic site with fire pits and fishing access to a stocked stream, near intersection of Rt. 9 & Co. Rt., 10. 518- 873-6777, www.lewisny.com

Material courtesy of David Blades, Town of Lewis Supervisor

Meadowmount was the the family home of women suffrugate, Inez Millholland. It is now the home of the Meadowmount School of Music. Classical concerts are held on Wednesday, Friday, and Sunday evenings during the summer at 1424 Co. Rt. 10. Mary McGowan, Administrative Director of Meadowmount School of Music

MINERVA

The Town of Minerva, located in the center of the Adirondacks, is a 162-square mile area in the southwest corner of Essex County. Most of its current population inhabit the hamlets of Minerva, Olmstedville, and Irishtown. It is 10 miles northeast of North Creek on Rt. 28N.

Minerva originated from the Totten and Crossfield purchase from the Native Americans in 1771. Francis Dominick is credited as being the first to have his land surveyed into lots, which is now the hamlets of Minerva and Olmstedville. Lieut. Ebenezer West and his five sons were among the first settlers within the hamlet of Minerva, around 1800. Family descendants are still living here today. William Hill came with his family to start a sawmill and gristmill in what is today the hamlet of Olmstedville. Early settlers of the town include the surnames of Leonard, Jones, Tallman, Talbot, Hawley, Gates, Provoncho, Brown, Ordway, Gardner, Bennett, Baker, Wilson, and Wamsley. In his narrative, *Twelve Years a Slave*, Solomon Northup states that he was born in Minerva. This area was initially part of the Town of Crown Point, then became part of Schroon in 1804, and finally the Town of Minerva was established on March 17, 1817.

Farming, lumber, potash, and tourism were the sources of income for this early community. Today, Minerva has less industry and fewer farms and stores, but tourism can still be considered an income potential.

THINGS TO DO

Donnelly Beach, on Minerva Lake, sports a campground and canoeing, hiking and snowmobiling trails. One can also canoe or kayak the Minerva Stream from Irishtown to Olmstedville, ending at Lavary Dam.

Hiking trails include the Moxham Mountain trailhead, off 14th Road, The Blue Ledges Trail off North Woods Club Road, The Boreas Loop, Cheney Pond to Irishtown via Lester Flow, and the Vanderwhacker Mountain Trailhead off Rt. 28N.

Minerva Town Hall is located at the point of Co. Rt. 30 and Rt. 28N. Here one can find a copy of the current Town Directory for business and services (also available online at www.townofminerva.com). Continuing north on 28N, pass over the Boreas River and take the trail to Vanderwhacker Fire Tower. Also, from Minerva, travel down Longs Hill Rd. to Irishtown, site of an early settlement that now contains a one-room schoolhouse and Saint Mary's Catholic Church (1842), now an oratory. William Byrne, one of the 25 men credited for capturing John Wilkes Booth, is buried in St. Mary's cemetery.

The history of our town can be enjoyed at the Minerva Historical Society museum located in Olmstedville on Co. Rt. 29; open during the summer months. Here one can view copies of art by Winslow Homer, a frequent visitor to the town. For more info, visit the Historical Society website at www.irishtown.com.

Minerva Day Celebration is an all-day, town-wide event, including fishing derby, garage sales, parade, picnic and fireworks at Donnelly Beach. It normally occurs at the end of June. See the town website for annual date: www.townofminerva.com.

Another historic site is Aiden Lair. It was here on Sept. 14, 1901 that Theodore Roosevelt riding in a surrey stopped to change horses in his night ride from Mt. Marcy to North Creek to take the oath of president in Buffalo.

DATE: _____ WEATHER: _____

MEMORIES: _____

_____

_____

_____

_____

_____

_____

_____

_____

_____

_____

[Passport Stamp / Signature Here]

It is approx. 14 miles north of the village of Olmstedville on Rt. 28N.

Lodging, Food, Etc.:
Sullivan's. Groceries, gas, news, and books. Rts. 29 & 30, Olmstedville.

The Alpine Homestead B&B. 1314 Co. Rt. 29, Olmstedville. 518-251-4697

Betty's Funny Farm/B&B. 676 14th Rd., Minerva. 518-251-2929

Morningside Camps & Cottages. 67 Longs Hill Rd.,Omlstedville. 866-210-2694

Mountain Niche Antiques (closed November thru May). 2143 Rt. 28N, Minerva. 518-251-2566

Hornbeck Boats. Canoes and kayaks. 141 Trout Brook Rd., Olmstedville 518-251-2764

Lil' Nony's Bakery & Sandwich Shop. Baked goods, breakfast, and lunch. Open Mother's Day weekend thru Columbus Day. 1385 Co. Rt. 29, Olmstedville. 518-251-2289

St. Mary's Catholic Church, built in 1847 in Irishtown. Vincent Cangelosi

Owl at Twilight. Latin/Spanish restaurant. Open seasonally during the summer months. 1322 Co. Rt. 29, Olmstedville. 518-251-4696

The Kitchen at Sporty's Iron Duke Saloon. 1723 Rt. 28N, Minerva. 518-251-5260

Material courtesy of Teresa Brannon Haley, Town of Minerva Historian & Joy Healy

131

MORIAH TOWN & PORT HENRY VILLAGE

The Town of Moriah is in eastern Essex County on the shore of Lake Champlain, approx. 18 miles north of Ticonderoga, and in the eastern Adirondack Park. The town consists of the Village of Port Henry and six hamlets: Moriah, Mineville, Witherbee, Moriah Center, Grover Hills, Moriah Corners. The current population is approx. 4,880.

HISTORY

Moriah was first settled in 1785 and the town was formed in 1808 from the Town of Elizabethtown. The town's industrialized past is evident in the landscape and in its buildings. Moriah, was a boom and bust town. When the iron arrived, it turned Port Henry, situated on Lake Champlain, into a booming transport terminal. The railroad and Lake Champlain barge routes transported goods to market. Until the great open pit mines of the West were developed, Moriah was a capital of the mining industry.

In its early history, a mill was first built in Port Henry in 1766 with the first permanent settlement in 1785. Several large companies operated mines in the town, the best remembered is the Witherbee, Sherman Company, whose magnificent headquarters in Port Henry are now used for the town offices.

Timber harvesting and land clearing in the first half of the 19th Century occurred at a great rate as there were 20 sawmills on the river between Ensign Pond and Lake Champlain. Docks were built at Port Henry as early as 1820. Lumber was rafted north to Canada, and, when the Champlain Canal opened, to southerly markets.

Moriah attracted immigrants of many

nationalities to work in the mines. It remains one of the most populated towns on Essex County. Moriah's industrial past is still evident, reflected in the industrial park located there today and in the tourist industry which is developing around the industry's artifacts. The story of its mining past is being collected and exhibited at the Iron Center Museum in Port Henry and at the Essex County Historical Society in Elizabethtown.

RECREATION

Hike:
Cheney Mountain, Crowfoot Pond Trail, and Hammond Pond Wilderness.

Kayak:
Lake Champlain, Lincoln Pond, Newport Pond, and Bartlett Pond.

Fish:
Lake Champlain is one of the best bass lakes in America.

Historic Sites:
Iron Center Museum is housed in the historic laboratory of the Witherbee, Sherman Mining Co. Open mid-June to mid-October. 34 Park Place, Port Henry. 518-546-3587

Town Hall. This magnificent building is the former headquarters of the Witherbee, Sherman Co. The building is now used for town offices. 38 Park Place, Port Henry.

Mining wealth has left Moriah with a large number of architecturally significant historic buildings. Walking tour brochures are available at Town Hall and Iron Center Museum.

Terminal Dock is one of the two largest piers on Lake Champlain. Dock Lane, Port Henry.

DATE: _____ WEATHER: _____

MEMORIES: _____

_____

_____

_____

_____

_____

_____

_____

_____

_____

_____

_____

_____

_____

[Passport Stamp / Signature Here]

Sherman Free Library. A must see. This beautiful 1887 building was designed by architect S. Gifford Slocum. Its slate roofs, portico arch and semi-circular window transoms express an English Victorian aesthetic suited to a college campus. 20 Church St., Port Henry.

Belfry Fire Tower. Take Rt. 4 from Port Henry to Moriah Center. Then continue north on Rt. 70 to Witherbee and continue 0.3 mile to gate and trail on left.

Champ, the reputed Lake Champlain Monster. Area residents and visitors claim to have seen a monster in Lake Champlain that is similar to Scotland's Loch Ness monster. Bring some binoculars, a camera and go monster spotting on one of the bluffs above the lake!

Visit www.porthenrymoriah.com for more!

The Iron Center Museum is in the Witherbee, Sherman Mining Co. laboratory in Port Henry. Tim Bryant

Material courtesy of Tim Bryant, Moriah Chamber of Commerce

133

NEWCOMB

The Town of Newcomb is located in western Essex County in the very heart of the Adirondack Park. It is about 25 miles due west of the Northway (I-87) exit 29, about 120 miles north of Albany. Newcomb is about 200 square miles with much of the land designated wild forest, wilderness, and historic sites. Geographic features include Santanoni Mountain and many lakes and ponds. The town contains the hamlets of Newcomb and Tahawus Club.

HISTORY

The town was settled around 1816. Most of the early industry was devoted to harvesting lumber until the discovery of large iron ore deposits. The Town of Newcomb was established in 1828 from parts of the towns of Minerva and Moriah. By the end of the 19th Century, the town was becoming famous as a sportsman's paradise. Theodore Roosevelt was informed of the impending death of President William McKinley in September 1901 while hunting and hiking in the town, and actually became President in Newcomb, while on his way to North Creek, where he took the oath of office.

INTERESTING PLACES TO VISIT

Newcomb is one of the most scenic spots in the Adirondacks and boasts many attractions.

Santanoni Great Camp transports visitors to the Gilded Age of roughing it in style. It is free and open to the public on a well-maintained 5-mile carriage road. During the winter months, the trail becomes a popular cross-country skiing and snowshoe trail. www.aarch.org/santanoni/santanoni.html

The Adirondack Interpretive Center is just west of the hamlet on Rt. 28N and has miles of walking trails, an interpretive building, and regular educational programming. www.esf.edu/aic

Town Beach and Picnic Area is a beautiful spot on Lake Harris just off Rt. 28N. During the summer months lifeguards are on duty. The beach is free and open to the public.

High Peaks Golf Course is a scenic par-32 9-hole course that is open to the public.

Newcomb Town Overlook Park is a roadside park with a vista of the Adirondack High Peaks, parking, and picnic area on Rt. 28N.

Mount Adams fire tower: From the hamlet of Newcomb go east on 28N for approx. 6 miles to intersection of Rt. 2 on left. Then go approx. 2 miles on Rt. 2 to Rt. 25 on left. Follow Rt. 25 and signs to "Marcy and the High Peaks." After driving 2.8 miles you will see a large blast furnace on the right. Continue for 0.2 mile, where you will find a parking area on the right. It is a 2.4-mile hike to the summit.

Village of Tahawus and High Peaks Trailheads include the restored Blast Furnace at Tahawus, the McNaughton Cottage where Teddy Roosevelt stayed in 1901. It is on Co. Rt. 25 in the north part of the town. This was the site of a major mining and iron smelting operation in the 19th Century. It is now a ghost town. www.ghosttowns.com/states/ny/tahawusoradirondak.html

Goodnow Mountain fire tower (60'!): Go approx. 4 miles west of the hamlet of Newcomb on 28N. Trailhead is on the left.

Hiking, canoeing, and snowmobile trails exist

DATE: _____ WEATHER: _____

MEMORIES: _____

_____

_____

_____

_____

_____

_____

_____

_____

_____

_____

_____

_____

_____

[Passport Stamp / Signature Here]

throughout the town. Recent state purchases of land have opened wild forest and wilderness areas that have been closed to the general public for decades. www.newcombny.com

Material courtesy of George H. Canon, Town Supervisor

A breathtaking view from the Goodnow fire tower of Rich Lake and the High Peaks in the distance. Bob Lilly

NORTH ELBA

The Town of North Elba is in northwestern Essex County two hours north of Albany in the beautiful northern Adirondacks. It is 40 miles southwest of Plattsburg. The town contains the Village of Lake Placid and the western part of the Village of Saranac Lake, and the hamlets of North Elba, Ray Brook, Undercliff, and Whiteface. There are also three lakes: Mirror, Placid, and Round.

HISTORY

The first settlers arrived in the early 1800s, however due to the "Year Without a Summer" caused by a volcano eruption in the Pacific and poor mining conditions, North Elba was not established as a town until 1850.

One of the most famous residents of the town was John Brown who was attracted by the views of Gerrit Smith, a local abolitionist who came to the town in 1849. Smith founded a community for former black slaves but the area was not suitable for family farms and the effort failed.

John Brown (1800-1859) brought his wife and seven children to a 244-acre farm in 1849 at North Elba where he planned to aid the free blacks living in Timbuctoo, a farming community. In the winter of 1857-58, Brown joined the abolitionist movement in Kansas, leaving his family behind to maintain their farm. John returned occasionally to check on them. In the summer of 1859 he went to Virginia and on October 16th he led a raid on the US Arsenal at nearby Harpers Ferry to get arms for a slave insurrection. Brown was captured after the raid and executed in December. His wife brought his body back to the Adirondacks. Today, tourists visit Brown's farm and his grave, a NYS Historic site.

Another famous resident was Melvil Dewey (1851-1931), founder of the American Library Association and inventor of the Dewey Decimal System for classifying books. He first came to the Adirondacks in the 1890s to relieve hay fever. He began the Lake Placid Club on Mirror Lake in the village of Lake Placid in 1895. Dewey only wanted the "best" people so only "prominent citizens" could apply. The club grew to cover two square miles with hotels, cottages, schools, tennis courts, golf courses, gardens, concert halls, stretches of wilderness, and its own fire department. Twenty-six farms provided fresh food for members. His son, Godfrey, promoted winter sports by making skating rinks, bringing ski instructors from Norway, and building a ski jump. Godfrey was credited with bringing the 1932 Winter Olympics to Lake Placid.

From a small farming community of 200, the town now has a summer population of over 8,000. Many people have built camps on Placid Lake as well as sprawling vacation homes.

POINTS OF INTEREST

Olympic Training Center. 421 Old Military Rd., Lake Placid. 518-523-2603

Olympic Torch Site. Located at the North Elba Horse Show Grounds, Rt. 73, Lake Placid.

Olympic Ski Jumping Complex. Rt. 73, Lake Placid.

Olympic Bobsled Run and Luge Venue. 220 Bobsled Rd., Lake Placid. 518-523-8203

Olympic Cross-Country Venue. Cascade Rd., Lake Placid

DATE: _____ WEATHER: _____

MEMORIES: _____

_____

_____

_____

_____

_____

_____

_____

_____

_____

_____

_____

_____

_____

[Passport Stamp / Signature Here]

John Brown's Farm and Burial Stone. 115 John Brown Rd., Lake Placid.

Uihlein Potato Farm & Sugar Maple Field Station, both operated by Cornell U. Their store is open occasionally and sells maple syrup and birch products. 281 & 157 Bear Cub Lane, Lake Placid. 518-523-9337

Adirondack LOJ, operated by Adirondack Mountain Club. 1002 Adirondack Loj Rd. www.adk.org

Craig Wood Golf Course. Rt. 73, Lake Placid

Whiteface Inn Golf Course. Whiteface Inn Rd., Lake Placid

Crowne Plaza/Lake Placid Club (2 courses). Olympic Hill, Lake Placid

Material courtesy of Beverley Reid, North Elba Historian

Take the road less traveled to two Cornell University research centers on Bear Cub Lane Road where you will find the Uihlein Potato Farm and Uihlein Sugar Maple Field Station. Their store (pictured above) is open occasionally and sells maple syrup and birch products. Mike Farrell

137

NORTH HUDSON

The Town of North Hudson is in south central Essex County 63 miles south of Plattsburgh. It has two hamlets: North Hudson and Underwood. The town was established in 1848 from the Towns of Moriah and Schroon. The name was derived from its proximity to the Hudson River. North Hudson is the second largest town in Essex County comprising 183.2 square miles of which, 68,055.76 acres are owned by the State of New York as part of the Adirondack Forest Preserve.

HISTORY

Settlers arrived in the early 1800s. The area was blessed with valuable pine and hemlock timbers. The hemlock bark was used in the tanning of leather. What is now the Blue Ridge Rd. saw many successful farms, mainly producing potatoes.

Because North Hudson was on an extremely busy stagecoach line, taverns and hotels became very profitable. Since the town had an extensive stream system water power kept numerous sawmills running.

Over the course of the 19th Century tourism began to take hold in North Hudson. Elk Lake and Underwood began to attract people from other parts of New York State as summer getaways. It was told (although never verified) that the Underwood Club was the location for some silent movies.

For over 47 years (1952-1981) North Hudson proudly boasted the popular theme park called Frontier Town which featured stagecoach rides, horse rides, action shows, and rodeos.

North Hudson is now visited by hunters, fisherman, snowmobilers and hikers. The town's principal peaks are Gore Mountain

(formerly Dix Mountain) and Nipple Top. There are numerous ponds in town; Elk Lake, Boreas Pond, Clear Pond, Deadwater Pond, Johnson's Pond, and Wolf Pond. With NYS owning over 68,000 forever wild acres, North Hudson will always be a place for nature lovers.

Camping, Lodging, Etc.:
Campers can find many places to put head to pillow. The Sharpe Bridge State Campground, one of the two oldest campsites in the state, is located on the west shore of the Schroon River with 40 campsites. There are picnic tables and visitors can go fishing or hiking. Directions: From (I-87), take Exit 30. Then turn left and proceed 3 miles to campground on left.

Yogi Bear at Paradise Pines Camping is located along the Schroon River and has 157 campsites, cabins, and yurts. 4035 Blue Ridge Rd., North Hudson.

Blue Ridge Falls Campsite has 76 campsites and is at 3438 Blue Ridge Rd. Relax and take a swim at our river beach or enjoy lunch at the town's picnic area.

The first Saturday in May, North Hudson hosts an Antique Car Show. Walk around and listen to the owners explain and brag about the beautifully conditioned cars.

Going up the Blue Ridge Rd., keep your eyes open for the balanced rock that nature placed there. Eat delicious baked goods at The Buffalo Farm while watching the buffalo roam. 3187 Blue Ridge Rd., North Hudson.

Off the Blue Ridge Rd. is Elk Lake Lodge. *Outside* magazine ranked it one of the "10 Best Wilderness Lodges in North America." 1106 Elk Lake Rd., North Hudson. www.elklakelodge.com

DATE: _____ WEATHER: _____

MEMORIES: _____

_____

_____

_____

_____

_____

_____

_____

_____

_____

_____

_____

_____

_____

_____

[Passport Stamp / Signature Here]

With breathtaking views and a myriad of outdoor activities, North Hudson is a destination for all seasons.

Material courtesy of Joe Provoncha, Town of North Hudson Historian

At the Adirondack Buffalo Farm you can watch buffalo roam and purchase baked goods, homegrown vegetables, buffalo meat products, gifts, and books. Doreen Ossenkop

139

SCHROON

The Town of Schroon is in southern Essex County, east of Ticonderoga in the eastern part of the Adirondack Park. It includes these hamlets: Schroon Lake, Severance, Paradox, South Schroon Lake, and Loch Muller.

During the 1700s French soldiers and officers were encamped at Fort St. Frederick at Crown Point. Begun as a military post in 1730 and completed in 1736, the fort served to protect French fur trade interests against the English. While exploring the Great Wilderness region or North Woods these very same soldiers discovered the lake. It is said that the officers gave the name SCARRON to the picturesque lake in memory of the widow of the French dramatist and poet, Paul Scarron. This poor crippled poet was enlightened by the grace of his young and beautiful wife who after his death secretly married Louis XIV. Schroon Lake may very well take its name from Madame Scarron. The name Schroon has been a subject of distortion over the years by its very own settlers. The town's name Scarron remained on record until 1837.

The Town of Schroon was settled about 1797. It was formed from Crown Point, March 20, 1804.

The three major industries of the town were tanneries, gristmills, and sawmills. In 1835 there were 45 sawmills in the confines of the town and by 1855 the population of the town was 2085, a number never reached in modern times. One sawmill in particular was built at the foot of Paradox Lake by Joseph Richards, and a gristmill by David Stowell.

Another important industry centered on the manufacture of leather from the many tanneries that existed throughout the town.

The hemlock forests provided the bark necessary for the production of the leather. The Schroon Lake Tannery was established by Lorenzo Hall in 1852. Iron ore was found in the town and a forge was built before 1830 at the Schroon falls by Horace Hall.

Many hotels and boarding houses were in full operation in the town between 1875 and 1910. The first Leland House was built in 1872 on a 6-acre parcel by Thomas Leland. It accommodated nearly 300 quests. Trout and venison were main items on the menu. The Ondawa Hotel, Groove Point House, Bogle & Silbert Boarding houses, and the Schroon Lake House were most popular in the town. The Effingham and the Evelyn, one of several steamboats on the lake, would transport guests to their respective accommodations from Pottersville where they would board after traveling by stagecoach from the train station in Riparius.

Today the town of Schroon (Scarron) is a popular resort town enhanced by its beautiful 9-mile lake which attracts many visitors during the summer and winter months. Its many fine shops and restaurants on Main Street offer unique arts and crafts and family style cooking.

POINTS OF INTEREST

Schroon-North Hudson Historical Society Museum, special collections of Schroon and North Hudson artifacts and memorabilia. 1144 Rt. 9, Schroon Lake.

Town Park, along Schroon Lake with 700 feet of prime sandy beach for your enjoyment along with tennis courts, the Boathouse Theatre, and the 4th of July spectacular parade and fireworks.

140

DATE: _____ WEATHER: _____

MEMORIES: _____

_____

_____

_____

_____

_____

_____

_____

_____

_____

_____

_____

_____

_____

[Passport Stamp / Signature Here]

Seagle Music Colony is the oldest summer vocal training program in the US with performances in July and August.
999 Charlie Hill Rd., Schroon Lake.
www.seaglecolony.org

The Adirondack Marathon is a major event in the fall whereby runners circle the lake.

Snowmobiling is popular, with miles of trails throughout the town.

There is a Fishing Derby that's sponsored by the Fish & Game Club.

Towne Store. 1089 Main St., Schroon Lake.

Pitkins Restaurant. 1085 Main St., Schroon Lake.

Visit the Chamber of Commerce building on Main Street for all the daily activities.

The Schroon Lake Town Park, has a 700-foot sandy beach, tennis courts, the Boathouse Theatre, and the 4th of July spectacular parade and fireworks. Gary Glebus

Material courtesy of Gary Glebus, Town of Schroon Historian

TICONDEROGA

The Town of Ticonderoga is often referred to as the "Land between the waters." It is located at the confluence of Lake George and Lake Champlain in the southeastern corner of Essex County. Ten million years ago, part of the flat coastal plain which is now the Lake Champlain valley began to rise. It's still rising. Ticonderoga drops down to that lake, and rises up to Eagle Lake. The town includes these hamlets: Ticonderoga, South Ti, Streetroad, Chilson, and Baldwin.

NOTABLE SITES

Lake Champlain: Connecting New York, Vermont, and Canada the lake, once a transportation hub, now primarily used for fishing and recreation. The Fort Ti road will take you down to the Ti ferry landing and the boat launch.

Lake George: Called "Queen of America's Lakes" this clear spring-fed 32-mile long lake nestled 220 feet higher than Lake Champlain is noted for boating, fishing, and diving on its countless shipwrecks. Three access roads lead to the lake: The Portage South, Water St. South, and Baldwin Rd. South. All three dead end on various mountains.

Rogers Rock: Dominating Lake George's northern end and overlooking Ticonderoga's beach is what some call Rogers Slide. Take the Portage South (uphill) in Ti and follow along when it becomes Black Point road to the beach.

Eagle Lake: Higher yet and surrounded by secluded camps and hiking trails. Here you feel the mountains while time slows down. Take Rt. 74 West into the mountains from Ti.

Fort Ticonderoga: "America's Fort." Built

by the French in the 1750s, captured by the British in 1759, and called at the time, "Key to a Continent." Here the 1700s and 1800s come to life as you walk through the hallowed halls of the Great Stone Fortress. From Rt. 22, turn right on Fort Ticonderoga Rd. at the stop signs. 30 Fort Ti Rd.

Ticonderoga Historical Society, "The Hancock House": This colonial restoration and research library presents programs that display Ticonderoga's rich history. The business district in Ti runs from "The Monument" traffic circle in front of the Historical Society, to the 1888 building (The Heritage Museum). The distance is about one mile. (Moses Circle)

Ticonderoga Heritage Museum: Ti has been a mill town for most of its history. International Paper's Mill 10 still operates in the town and Ticonderoga Pencils once dotted every child's desk. Explore that history as you watch Lake George's water fall the last few feet down to Lake Champlain level. 137 Montcalm St.

The Community Building: Home of Ticonderoga's government, and a gift from Horace Moses, one of Ti's favorite sons. Located near the 1888 building in the East part of the hamlet area, here is your place for maps, permits and the like. 132 Montcalm, St.

Hiking and exercise trails: Cooks Mountain trail (off Baldwin Rd.) revisits the days of Robert Rogers and New France. The LaChute river walk takes you past narrative plaques explaining man's use of the river. 137 Montcalm St.

Material courtesy of Fred Provoncha, Technical Director of the Ticonderoga Heritage Museum

DATE: _____ WEATHER: _____

MEMORIES: _____

_____

_____

_____

_____

_____

_____

_____

_____

_____

_____

_____

_____

_____

_____

_____

[Passport Stamp / Signature Here]

The Ticonderoga Heritage Museum portrays the industrial history of Ticonderoga and surrounding areas including graphite mining, Dixon Pencil, paper making, and the impact of the industrial development on the people and their town. Ticonderoga Heritage Museum

WESTPORT

The Town of Westport, on Lake Champlain in Northwest Bay, is 4 miles east of I-87, exit 31. The town is in the northeastern part of Essex County approx. 42 miles south of Plattsburgh. It contains two hamlets, Westport and Wadhams.

In 1764, William Gilliland surveyed the area, naming his land tract Bessboro, after his daughter. First settled in 1770, with a sawmill just south of the bay, the property was abandoned during the Revolutionary War. In 1785, the Barber family, from CT, farmed land where Barber's Point lighthouse is located and where descendants currently operate the Barber Homestead Campground. The first permanent structure, Halstead Tavern, built in 1800, was located at the top of the Washington St. hill on the corner of Main St.

From 1850 to 1885, Westport was home to three blast furnaces when high quality iron ore was extracted from nearby mountains. The remains of one furnace can be seen at Normandie Beach Club (Furnace Point Rd.).

In 1859, abolitionist John Brown's body came through Westport on the Barber's Point sail ferry on the way to his burial on his Lake Placid farm.

Since the early 19th Century, Westport was a portal to the Adirondack Mountains and Elizabethtown, the county seat. As commercial steamboat traffic declined after World War II, people turned to pleasure craft. The side-paddle-wheeler steamboat Ticonderoga, preserved at Vermont's Shelburne Museum since 1954, used to overnight in Westport.

These are the commodities that were commercially produced: dairy, bird's foot trefoil, corn, wheat, and sunflowers for seeds.

Hay is still a major crop. Several community supported agriculture farmers have customers come to their farm to pick up their vegetables and maple syrup. Others take their goods to local farmers' markets. Apples, grapes, heritage beef, chicken, and pork products are produced locally. DaCy Meadow Farm features farm-to-table dining and hospitality. Rolling Hills Farm is designed to provide a back-to-the-land vacation experience for its members. Champlain Valley Milling grinds specialty organic flours from numerous grains.

Arts and culture: Painting, pottery, poetry, prose, sculpture, weaving, felting, theatre, dance, music, lectures, book clubs, films, yoga, massage, and a love of basketball are all part of Westport's life style.

PLACES TO VISIT

Westport Heritage House, features art shows and a short historic video offering stories and directions during summer hours. 6459 Main St., Rt. 9N. 518-962-4805

Ballard Park Concerts, on Thursday nights in July and August.

CATS - Champlain Area Trail System. 518-962-2287, www.champlainareatrails.com

Depot Theatre at 6705 Main St., Westport. 518-962-4449

Bouquet River Theatre Festival, children's theater. 518-412-2525

Contact Elizabeth Lee, outdoor guide, for an interpreted nature hike. 518-962-4765

Meadowmount School of Music has aspiring young violinists and cellists offering bi-weekly summer concerts. 518-962-2400

DATE: _____ WEATHER: _____

MEMORIES: _____
_____
_____
_____
_____
_____
_____
_____
_____
_____
_____ [Passport Stamp / Signature Here]

Westport Country Club offers views of the Adirondack Mountains, Lake Champlain, and Vermont's Green Mountains.

Dotted around the bay are three summer restaurants. Lake access includes a resort, boat launch site, full-service marina with boat and kayak rentals, and a swimming beach.

Historic Sites:
Inn at Westport (1877) at 1234 Stevenson Rd.

Westport Hotel and Tavern (1877) at 6691 Main St.

Visit the Fair Grounds, home of the longest lasting Fair in NYS, at 3 Sisco St.

Camp Dudley (1885), a YMCA boys camp, the oldest continuous boys camp in the country. 126 Camp Dudley Rd.

Westport Library has a cozy stone fireplace. Located in the town center.

Wadhams is 5 minutes north on Rt. 22 of the hamlet of Westport. It features waterfalls by the library (763 NYS Route 22), a century-old electric power plant, and a wood-fired artisan

bakery in a former agricultural supply store!

Dogwood Bread Company. 2576 Co. Rt. 10, Wadhams. www.dogwoodbread.com

For more information, visit westportny.com.

Material courtesy of Dee Carroll, President of Westport Chamber of Commerce

The beautiful Westport Library, built in 1888 in the center of town, where in the winter you will enjoy the cozy warmth of its stone fireplace. Dee Carroll

145

WILLSBORO

The Town of Willsboro is located in the northeastern part of Essex County on the shore of Lake Champlain. The town covers an area of 72 sq. mi. and has a year-round population of nearly 2,000. During the summer months this population is more than doubled with seasonal residents. The town includes these hamlets: Willsboro, Reber, and Willsboro Point.

Willsboro was first settled in 1765 by William Gilliland, a well-to-do Irish merchant from New York City, who had purchased land grants along Lake Champlain from soldiers who did not desire to settle on their grants. The town was formed on March 7, 1788 from the old town of Crown Point. The original spelling was Willsborough, which was officially shortened to Willsboro in 1906.

During the Revolutionary War there was an eight-year period when Willsborough was abandoned. The resettlement began in 1784 and it rapidly grew into a thriving community. By the early 1800s there was a gristmill, several sawmills, an iron works, an established school system dating from 1787, a tannery in 1818, several inns and taverns as well as two stores. By 1810 the population had grown to 663 people and by 1825 had increased to 1,166. In 1875 the New York and Canada Railroad was built through Willsborough changing the mode of transportation and commerce from the steamers and canal boats on the lake to the railroad. In 1879 a pulp mill was built near the falls on the Boquet River and by the year 1882 was fully operational and employed about 150 men, 80 of those worked in the forests cutting the pulpwood for the mill. During this period there were two fairly large hotels. The Riverside is in the downtown area and the Bayview House near the railroad station.

In 1883 there was also a large hotel on the end of Willsboro Point which was accessed by both steamers and a stagecoach which ran between the railroad station and the hotel called the "Green Mt. View House," later the "Willsborough."

The early 1900s saw the beginning of the summer tourist business with summer homes being built along the lake shore, as well as summer youth camps being started. The first was Camp Poko-Moonshine as a boys camp and that evolved into a co-ed camp now called Poko-McCready. In 1915 the Paine family built a private 9-hole golf course and today it is open to the public.

In 1953 the Cabot Corporation built a large manufacturing facility which produced a product from the mineral wollastonite which is mined locally. This product is sold in various grades of pulverized mineral which is used primarily as a bonding agent in pottery, plywood, wallboard, porcelain, paints, etc. They employ about 160 people. We also have another large industrial building which houses three businesses. We have a new high school, a NYS boat launch, a bank, a library, two senior housing facilities, a drugstore, two gas stations, two stores, a bowling alley, and five eating establishments.

PLACES TO VISIT

Homestead (1812). Located about two miles north of Willsboro. 4403 Rt. 22. www.pokomac.com

Adsit Log Cabin (1795). Located about four miles onto Willsboro Point.

Willsboro Heritage Society Museum. Next to the library. www.willsboroheritage.org

DATE: _____ WEATHER: _____

MEMORIES: _____

_____

_____

_____

_____

_____

_____

_____

_____

_____

_____

_____

_____

_____

[Passport Stamp / Signature Here]

Pain Memorial Free Library. 2 Gilliland Lane, Willsboro.

Recreation:
Boating, canoeing, snowmobiling, and hiking are popular. There are public tennis courts, a golf course, and a bowling alley. Salmon fishing is good on the Boquet River in the spring and fall as well as ice fishing on Long Pond and Lake Champlain.

Material courtesy of Ron Bruno, Town of Willsboro Historian

The Adsit Log Cabin (1795) was built on Willsboro Point by Samuel Adsit. He came to Willsboro after he had fought in the American Revolution and built the cabin for his family of sixteen. Ron Bruno

147

WILMINGTON

The Town of Wilmington is located in the Adirondack Mountains of northern New York State at the foot of majestic Whiteface Mountain on the West Branch of the Ausable River. Rt. 86 is the main road through town.

Wilmington, established in 1822, was first populated circa 1800 by hardy pioneer farmers from New England. Gristmills, sawmills, and distilleries sprang up along the river. Reuben Sanford, arriving in 1803, was the first industrialist in Wilmington, building a potash factory, a starch factory, and an ironworks. From the 1820s to the 1880s lumbering operations in the Wilmington area provided charcoal to supply iron mining and forge operations. As the iron industry shifted westward, lumbering provided for the area's pulp and paper-making industry. In 1901, the Haselton Lumber Company opened to produce wood products.

The West Branch of the Ausable River and other local ponds and streams provided fish for the early settlers, later becoming sport for tourists. Many Adirondack hunting and fishing guides plied their trade in the Wilmington area. Hoteliers also supported guides to lead visitors on local mountain trails. Professional photographers introduced the scenic attractiveness of the area to the rest of the world with photographs of Whiteface Mountain, High Falls Gorge, and Wilmington Notch. The area gradually gained a reputation as a scenic resort.

As the 19th Century drew to an end, the iron forges closed due to mid-west competition, and emphasis began to shift from traditional industry and farming to tourism. Wilmington entered the golden age of hotels, tourist cottages, and Adirondack-style camps.

Whiteface Mountain Veteran's Memorial Highway was dedicated in 1935 to the veterans of WWI by President Franklin Delano Roosevelt, becoming one of New York State's most popular attractions.

By the 1940s, downhill skiing became a significant new winter sport and Whiteface Mountain Ski Center was inaugurated, first at Marble Mountain, then in 1958 at the current site. Whiteface Mountain was the venue for the alpine ski events for the 1980 Winter Olympics.

In the late 1940s, Julian Reiss created Santa's Workshop, purported to be the first theme park of its kind in America. Motels sprang up all over town to accommodate all the visitors.

By the 1960s, the West Branch of the Ausable River was touted as a world-class fishing stream, thanks in large part to Wilmington's fly-fishing author and promoter, Fran Betters.

From its rural roots, Wilmington has evolved into an outdoor recreation, science, and education destination featuring its natural attributes. The unique blend of natural resources, nearby wilderness, entrepreneurship, and personal enterprise has created a small rural town of national and international acclaim.

ATTRACTIONS & THINGS TO DO

Whiteface Mountain Veterans Memorial Highway. Drive to the top of the mountain for scenic views and birding. Rt. 431. www.whiteface.com

Whiteface Mountain Ski Center. Ski Whiteface Mountain in winter, Gondola ride to top of Little Whiteface in summer,

DATE: _____ WEATHER: _____

MEMORIES: _____

_____

_____

_____

_____

_____

_____

_____

_____

_____

_____

_____

[Passport Stamp / Signature Here]

mountain bike Whiteface summer & fall. 5021 Rt. 86. www.whiteface.com

High Falls Gorge. Scenic walk over & adjacent to the West Branch of the Ausable River. Rt. 86. www.highfallsgorge.com

Santa's Workshop, Kiddie Park (summer through fall and Christmas previews). Whiteface Memorial Highway Rt. 431. www.northpoleny.com

Wilmington Wildlife Refuge & Rehabilitation Center. Visitors welcome! Springfield Road. www.adirondackwildlife.org

Fishing the West Branch of the Ausable River. www.ausableflyfishing.com

Wilmington-Lake Everest Town Beach. Swimming/canoeing/kayaking/picnicking. Bowman Lane.

Wilmington mountain biking and hiking trails. Free maps available at Visitors Bureau. www.whitefaceregion.com

Wilmington Historical Society. www.wilmingtonhistoricalsociety.org

Material courtesy of Karen Peters, Wilmington Historical Society & Michelle Burns, Whiteface Mountain Visitors Bureau

The Whiteface Mountain Veteran's Memorial Highway was dedicated in 1935 to the veterans of WWI by President Franklin Delano Roosevelt. The view from the summit (4,865') is breathtaking. Olympic Regional Development Authority, Wilmington Historical Society

149

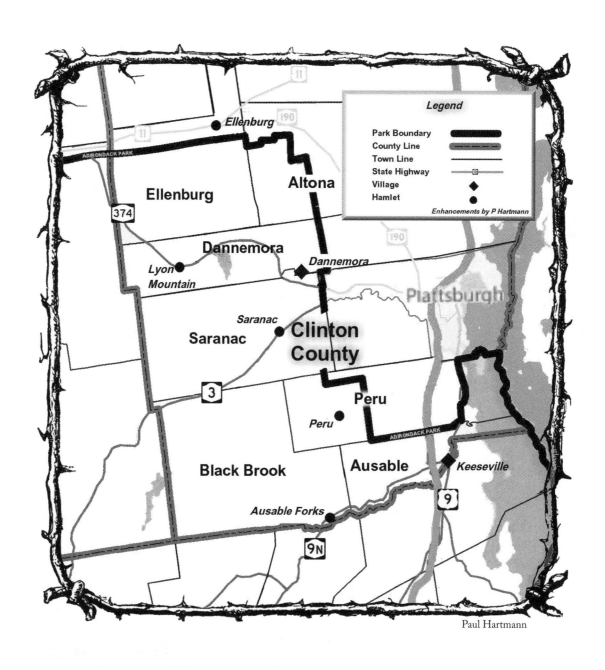

Ellenburg

Altona

Ellenburg

Dannemora

Lyon Mountain

Dannemora

Saranac

Saranac

Clinton County

Plattsburgh

Peru

Peru

Black Brook

Ausable

Keeseville

Ausable Forks

Legend

Park Boundary
County Line
Town Line
State Highway
Village
Hamlet

Enhancements by P Hartmann

Paul Hartmann

CHAPTER 5

REGION V:
CLINTON COUNTY

ALTONA

The Town of Altona covers 94 square miles in the northern part of Clinton County. It was formed on Dec. 2, 1857 from the Town of Chazy. The name originated from Altona, a suburb of Hamburg, Germany. It contains these hamlets: Altona, Crowley Corners, Dannemora Crossing, Forest, Irona, Jericho, Robinson, and Purdys Mills.

Altona is surrounded by the towns of Ellenburg, Chazy, Mooers, and Dannemora. On most days, one can see Lake Champlain, the Green Mountains of Vermont and the 3,809-foot high Lyon Mountain to the southwest from many parts of our town.

Our first settler (c.1850) is said to have been Simeon Wood. Soon after many others followed and settled along present-day Rt. 190 (also known as the Old Military Turnpike).

A railroad was one of the biggest assets to the Town back in the mid-1800s. Little villages were formed and known as Altona, Irona, Forest, Alder Bend, Jericho, Jerusalem, Purdy's Mills, and Sherlock Mills. There were a couple sawmills, a tannery factory, and a milk/cheese plant in town and they were powered by the Great Chazy River, which runs through the middle of Town and into Lake Champlain. (Lake Champlain borders New York and Vermont, and runs into the Province of Quebec.)

Feinberg Park is a small town-owned camping ground along the Great Chazy River where 50 camping sites are available for summer rentals. The Great Chazy River runs along the campground where fishing for brook trout has been very successful. There is a small beach area for swimming at 385 Devil's Den Rd. in Altona. The McGregor Powerhouse is also located here. It is one of the few surviving hydroelectric projects built by millionaire-philanthropist, William H. Miner who invented a railroad-car coupling device. The powerhouse supplied electricity to the Chazy school and town and his elaborate home, Heart's Delight farm. There is an effort to restore the brown, stucco-coated building, accented with dormers and three tall chimneys.

In the late 1800s and early 1900s, many residents made a living by picking blueberries on the famous, Flat Rock area approx. 13 miles NW of Plattsburgh and in the northern part of town. The selling price back then was about 3 cents per quart. At the time when I grew up (1970s) we would pick blueberries from 7 am to Noon and sell them for 75 cents per quart. Most of us picked 5-6 quarts in that time. Much of our school clothes and shoes were purchased with money from the sale of our berries. There is still a great crop each year and residents can be found picking blueberries on those hot summer days.

Altona Flat Rock Preserve is a good place to hike. It is at the end of Brunell Rd. in Altona.

We are now home to 65 wind turbines. Many landowners have leased their land to wind companies for the placement of turbines. This has been a huge project and has benefited all taxpayers in Altona as we receive stipends yearly for the 15-year contract. This has made it possible to improve the Town without a burden to taxpayers.

The Altona School was sold to New York State for a Correctional Facility back in the early 1980s after the district was merged to form Northern Adirondack Central School. This project created jobs with higher salaries and

DATE: _____ WEATHER: _____

MEMORIES: _____

_____

_____

_____

_____

_____

_____

_____

_____

_____

_____

_____

_____

_____

[Passport Stamp / Signature Here]

benefits for about 250 employees.

Most of our shopping is done in Plattsburgh, located 20 miles east. However the Town does have a Family Dollar, a couple of local general stores, and a very large banquet hall for weddings and other activities. The Rainbow Wedding and Banquet Hall has employed many locals for weekend events. The owners (Leonard and Jane Sample) have served up to 1500 individuals in a single afternoon.

The City of Montreal is less than an hour drive north of Altona. A two-hour drive south is historic Saratoga and only 20 minutes east of Town is Lake Champlain. To the west is the St. Lawrence River area where a popular gaming casino is located on the Akwasasne Indian Reservation.

Material courtesy of John Brunell, Town of Altona Assessor

The McGregor Powerhouse is located in Feinberg Park where there is fishing for brook trout and a small beach area for swimming in the Great Chazy River. The Power House is one of the few surviving hydroelectric projects built by millionaire-philanthropist, William H. Miner who invented a railroad-car coupling device. John Brunell

153

AUSABLE

This friendly town of AuSable is located on the west side of the Ausable River, in southern Clinton County, south of Plattsburgh, and is named after the Ausable River that flows through it and means "at the sand." The town includes the hamlets of Harkness, Clintonville, Keese Corners, Rogers, Thomasville, and the northern part of the Village of Keeseville.

Beginning in 1787, Quaker farmers established a permanent settlement at Union which is on the present boundary of the Towns of AuSable and Peru. They were farmers who grew wheat, corn, and potatoes, but later to supplement their income they branched out to a lumber and potash trade in Plattsburgh and southern Quebec. The Union Village built the first schoolhouse as well as stores, blacksmith shop, taverns, and a religious meetinghouse. The harsh climate, rugged terrain, thin and stony soils made agriculture difficult.

During the first half of the 1800s the discovery of iron had a great effect on the settlement of the area. One of the most significant of the mining operators was the Peru Iron Company which created the mining and manufacturing village of Clintonville. It developed into a productive iron community. By 1845 it boasted an iron industrial complex that produced over 1600 tons of iron and 1800 tons of nails annually. Over 2000 people lived in the village and surrounding area.

The Town of AuSable was formed in 1839. By this time, the iron-manufacturing boom was in full swing.

By the 1870s the area's importance in iron production was slipping away to bigger mines in the western United States. The decline of the iron industry in the AuSable Valley signaled the end of the area's growth and development. It was replaced by wood products industry and the increasing tourism industry.

Then with the construction of I-87 it bypassed Keeseville and the Town of AuSable. People purchasing vacation homes in the area later followed this and the town has become a bedroom community for the new Plattsburgh businesses that replaced the Plattsburgh Air Force Base.

POINTS OF INTEREST

Keystone Arch Bridge: One of the oldest standing arch bridges in the U.S. As master mason, Solomon Towsend, was constructing the bridge in the spring of 1842 heavy rain and flooding of the Ausable River undermined the project causing the partially built arch, falsework and rubble fill to fall into the river This did not deter Townsend who completed the bridge in 1843. The bridge has a span of 110 feet and has continuously carried traffic since that date. It can be reached by taking I-87 to Exit 34. Take Rt. 9N to the traffic light at Main St. (Rt. 22) in the Hamlet of AuSable and turn right. The bridge is at the bottom of the hill. It connects the town of AuSable and the village of Keeseville.

Ausable Chasm: Descend hundreds of feet and walk on natural stone trails above the Ausable River. One can also raft or tube downriver. 2144 Rt. 9, Ausable Chasm. www.ausablechasm.com

Lake Champlain Bikeways: Trails meander along quiet back roads through extraordinary mountain and countryside scenery. Try the Waters Edge Loop through AuSable. www.champlainbikeways.org/directions

Material courtesy of Roby Scott, Town of AuSable Historian

154

DATE: _____ WEATHER: _____

MEMORIES: _____

_____

_____

_____

_____

_____

_____

_____

_____

_____

_____

_____

_____

_____

_____

[Passport Stamp / Signature Here]

Beside this Adventure Trail (V-Bridge) at Ausable Chasm there are also natural stone walkways for the less daring. Ausable Chasm

155

BLACK BROOK

The Town of Black Brook is located in the SW corner of Clinton Co. and bordered on the east by the Town of Au Sable Forks. Black Brook is an important waterway in town. It contains these hamlets: Black Brook, Clayburg, Devins Corners, East Kilns, Hawkeye, Riverview, Rome, Stevens Landing, Swastika, Thomasville, Union Falls, and West Kilns.

In 1825 Zephania Palmer was possibly the first settler. On May 7, 1839 an act was passed forming the Town of Black Brook from part of the Town of Peru.

By 1828 iron ore was mined from deposits in Arnold Hill and a forge was constructed. By 1832 James and John Rogers bought out the entire iron holdings and formed the J & J Rogers Co. In June 1893 they constructed a pulp mill and in 1901 they built a paper mill. A railroad was constructed on the French Village Rd. to transport the paper to the main line. The paper mill closed in 1971 and a few buildings are still standing.

There are still some mines, but they are dangerous to enter. Over the years ice was taken from the mines for different functions.

The Palmer Hill fire tower (1930) was constructed to protect the nearby forests. It closed in 1988. It is privately owned and used for communications. Over the years it has been used as a picnic and blueberry picking spot.

INTERESTING PLACES TO VISIT

Riverside Hotel. Established in 1902, at the corner of McCrea St. & Rt. 9N. It has a great 8-lane bowling alley.

Outdoor Activites:
There are four bodies of water for fishing, boating, swimming, canoeing, camping, and hiking.

Fern Lake: Approx. 1 mile long and 4 miles northwest of the Town of Au Sable Forks. Fishing and boating is permitted.

Taylor Pond: 9 miles NW of Au Sable Forks on Route 9N at 1865 Silver Lake Rd. There is a NYS campsite on a 4-mile long, 813 acre "pond."

Silver Lake: Approx. 13 miles NW of Au Sable Forks. Follow Turnpike Rd. to Silver Lake Rd. About half of the surrounding land is owned by the state. Contains Douglas Resort & Campground (est. 1865).

Union Falls: A hamlet and pond on the western border with the Town of St. Armand.

Material courtesy of Rita Rongeau, Black Brook Town Historian

DATE: _____ WEATHER: _____

MEMORIES: _____

_____

_____

_____

_____

_____

_____

_____

_____

_____

_____

_____

_____

_____

_____

_____

[Passport Stamp / Signature Here]

Taylor Pond is the site of the DEC State campground on Rt. 9 N where campers, fishermen, and naturalists enjoy the primitive pond. There are also interior campsites on the 4-mile long pond. DEC

157

DANNEMORA TOWN

The Town of Dannemora is in the western section of Clinton Co in the northeastern Adirondack Mountains. It contains the village of Dannemora and the hamlet of Lyon Mountain. The name comes from the iron mining town of Dannemora in Sweden. The town was first settled around 1838 and formed in 1854 from the Town of Beekmantown.

Lyon Mountain was a small iron mining community located 30 miles from Plattsburgh on Rt. 374. The first iron ore was discovered by a trapper named Collins in 1823. Forty-five years later, the investors Foote, Meade, Weed, and Walds acquired possession of this property. Development started in 1873. Later, when the population reached 150, there were forty houses, a church, and a school. On June 8, 1874, the first railroad from Dannemora to Lyon Mountain started and was completed on Dec. 17, 1874. Then trains traveled the entire line with loads of iron all the way to Plattsburgh.

Republic Steel Co. took over the whole mining operation in 1937 and Lyon Mountain became the busiest place in Clinton Co. The population rose to approximately 4,000. Finally on June 30, 1967, the mining operation closed permanently.

The sport of baseball has been a longstanding tradition played in the hamlet of Lyon Mountain. In the 1880s the mining company started supporting a town team and the tradition is still being carried on today. The team is composed of adults who play in the summer months on a field built back in the 1930s by the mining company. Summer tourists from nearby lakes come out to support the team. Some of the Lyon Mountain boys have made it to the major leagues.

The Clinton Prison, or "Little Siberia," is in the Town of Dannemora. It is the largest and third oldest prison in NY. It was begun in 1845 to use convicts to mine and manufacture iron.

Today, Lyon Mountain is mostly retired people. Because it is located between Chateaugay Lake and Chazy Lake, it's a very enjoyable place to live. There is time to fish both in the summer and winter.

INTERESTING SIGHTS TO VISIT

Chazy Lake: Boasts 1,807 acres, and is 1.5 miles by 3.5 miles long. There is a DEC public boat launch on Rt. 374, five miles from the Village of Dannemora. The Town of Dannemora has a public beach open in the summer. The lake contains lake trout, landlocked salmon, rainbow trout, smallmouth bass, northern pike, brown bullhead, yellow perch, rainbow smelt, and pumpkinseed.

Chateaugay Lake: Boasts 545 acres, and is 5 miles by 2 miles long. Has Upper & Lower sections connected by what the locals call "The Narrows." Upper Chateaugay Lake is primarily within Dannemora Town lines. The DEC boat launch on this Lake is within the "Narrows" section in the Town of Ellenburg. The lake is 4 miles west of Lyon Mountain and the boat launch is 5 miles west of Lyon Mountain. The lake contains smallmouth bass, northern pike, yellow perch, brown bullhead, and pumpkinseed.

Lyon Mountain fire tower: Hiking to the tower is a very good adventure. From the summit on a clear day one can see all the way to Montreal, Canada. Directions: From the Village of Dannemora take Rt. 374 for approx. 9 miles to the end of Chazy Lake (Scenic Bay). Take your

DATE: _____ WEATHER: _____

MEMORIES: _____

_____

_____

_____

_____

_____

_____

_____

_____

_____

_____

_____

_____

_____

[Passport Stamp / Signature Here]

first left hand turn onto Chazy Lake Road and drive about 1.8 miles. Turn right onto a dirt road and drive about a mile to a parking area on the right.

Lyon Mountain Mining & Railroad Museum: Housed in the former Delaware and Hudson Railroad Station on Standish Road in Lyon Mountain. The museum is open from the first Saturday in June until the Saturday before Columbus Day on Wednesdays and Saturdays from 10 am – 2 pm. For more information, visit lyonmountainmuseum.blogspot.com.

Material courtesy of Ves Pivetta, Dannemora Town Historian & William H. Chase, Town of Dannemora Supervisor

Lyon Mountain Mining & Railroad Museum is housed in the former Delaware and Hudson Railroad Station on Standish Road in Lyon Mountain. Jill Jones, Bloated Toe Publishing

159

DANNEMORA VILLAGE

The Village of Dannemora is located in northern Clinton County in the foothills of the northeastern Adirondacks approx. 11 miles NW of the City of Plattsburg. Most of the Village is in the Town of Dannemora, but the southern part is in the Town of Saranac. The Village is named after an iron-mining town in Sweden.

Around 1831 iron ore was discovered near Chateaugay Lake a few miles northeast of the village which brought workers to the area. Thomas Hooker was the first permanent settler in 1838. On Dec. 14, 1854 the Town of Dannemora was formed from Beekmantown.

The Village of Dannemora grew up near Clinton Correctional Facility, which was established in 1845. Ransom Cook of Saratoga surveyed the area & chose a 200-acre parcel in the Town of Dannemora. Cook, the first warden, had workers clear the land & build a stockade and temporary buildings for officers, guards, workmen, and convicts. He went to Sing Sing and Auburn prisons and selected 50 strong and healthy convicts who were transported to Plattsburgh and then they walked the treacherous & steep trail in shackles, ankle-chains, and stripes. The bedraggled men arrived on June 3, 1845. The prisoners constructed a kitchen, blacksmith shop, steam sawmill, ore buildings, and an iron and brass foundry. Cook treated his prisoners with kindness and even dispensed with shackles & chains during work. The prison is sometimes called "Little Siberia," because of its remote northern location. It is the largest and third oldest prison in NYS.

Today approx. 1,250 workers are employed at Clinton Correctional Facility which houses approx. 2,700 inmates. The prison provides many jobs for nearby residents and its budget of about $33,600,000 per year is the lifeblood of the area.

POINTS OF INTEREST

Clinton Correctional Prison: As you travel through the Village on Rt. 374 you cannot miss the huge concrete walls and guard towers of the maximum security prison.

Recreation:
During the winter the Village has a rink for skating and hockey. There is also nearby Chateaugay Lake, a popular fishing attraction. Outfitters Plus on 1135 Cook St. provides fishing supplies.

Village of Dannemora Community Center: Contains the Dannemora Free Library. 40 Emmons St.

LaFontain Park: Provides family recreation activities on Smith St.

Places to Eat:
Stewarts Shops, Auggy's Pizza, China Wok, Dunkin Donuts, Haley's Pizza & Wings, Lashway's Meat Market & Deli, Maplefields, and Subway.

Visit www.villageofdannemora.com for more.

Material courtesy of Peter Light, Village of Dannemora Historian

DATE: _____ WEATHER: _____

MEMORIES: _____

_____

_____

_____

_____

_____

_____

_____

_____

_____

_____

_____

_____

[Passport Stamp / Signature Here]

Bird's-Eye View of Clinton Prison.   Dannemora, N. Y.

Early postcard photo of Clinton Prison in the Village of Dannemora.
T.B. Gilroy Collection

ELLENBURG

The Town of Ellenburg, located in the northwestern corner of Clinton County, is situated at the foothills of the northeastern Adirondack Mountains. It is approx. 25 miles northwest of Plattsburgh and contains these hamlets: Ellenburg Depot, Ellenburg Corners, Ellenburg Center, and Merrill. The town was named after landowner John R. Murray's daughter, Ellen.

The town has rolling, slanting, and mountainous land and its two major rivers empty into Lake Champlain. Many smaller brooks form the surface of Ellenburg. The town also shares 13-mile long Chateaugay Lake with the towns of Dannemora and Bellmont. Long established summer boarding camps for youth, Camp Jeanne D'arc for girls only and Camp Chateaugay, co-ed, are located on the western shore of the lake. NYSDEC has installed a public boat launch off Rt. 11 just north of Merrill. This launch is convenient for the many visiting for the great fishing.

Originally, Ellenburg was in Indian summer hunting grounds. In 1609, both France and England claimed a part of the area. In 1683, the Province of New York was divided into ten counties and Ellenburg was then in Albany County. By 1778 the counties had been renamed and realigned twice, now Ellenburg was in Clinton County. In 1831, the first town meeting was held and in 1832 the first road was built. The railroad reached Ellenburg in 1849 and in 1860 the first train went through from Rouses Point to Ogdensburg. The Military Turnpike, now Rt.190, connects with what is now Rt. 11.

Early industry was mainly farming, which led to the building of many dams for power that ran starch factories, creameries, tanning (leather) factories, gristmills, and sawmills as well as promoting numerous stores, blacksmith shops, schools, and churches.

Ellenburg has seen many changes. During the Cold War, Ellenburg became home to two missile silos operated out of the Plattsburgh Air Force Base. The missile sites operated from 1962 to 1965. When the missiles were removed the land was sold or rented. A private investor now owns both properties. One site became a home and office and the other a storage site. There are now two companies with windmill farms supplying electricity. The central school is newly remodeled and includes students of bordering townships.

Vital to the area are the Ellenburg Depot and Ellenburg Center fire departments for both fire response and rescue response.

Ellenburg is not only noted for great hunting and fishing but for the many old cemeteries and records for the genealogy seeker. Two of these are located Rt. 11.

For more information on local businesses: www.adirondacknorthcountry.com/ellenburg_directory_north_country.htm

Material courtesy of Hilda Danforth, former Town of Ellenburg Historian

DATE: _____ WEATHER: _____

MEMORIES: _____

_____

_____

_____

_____

_____

_____

_____

_____

_____

_____

_____

_____

_____

_____

_____

[Passport Stamp / Signature Here]

The West Hill Cemetery in Ellenburg had its first burial in 1832. It is pictured above, with wind farm turbines in the background. Hilda Danforth

PERU

Nestled between the Adirondack Mountains and Lake Champlain, the Town of Peru was formed from Plattsburgh and Willsborough on Dec. 28, 1792. A part of it was annexed back to Willsborough in 1799 and the towns of AuSable and Black Brook were taken off in 1839. The area of the town is approx. 79 square miles. Early settlers thought that the mountains surrounding the town resembled those of Peru, South America, hence, the origin of the town's name.

Harvesting timber became Peru's first industry, resulting in several sawmills along the Little Ausable River. A. Mason & Sons lumber mill flourished as the town's largest employer from 1883 to 1972. Now, the empty stone building is the only remnant of that once-busy mill site. This area is being converted for use as a public park for resident use.

As the lands were cleared of timber the area's rich, fertile soil gave rise to agriculture which persists to this day in the form of dairy farms and several large apple orchards. Iron making also played a major role in the economic development of early Peru with the discovery of high quality iron ore in the Arnold Hill area in 1810.

Peru has an exceptionally rich military history. Its Lake Champlain shores saw much activity during the French and Indian War. The lake was the main north-south corridor for Native Americans and French and British armies. Benedict Arnold's most important Revolutionary War naval engagement with the British at the Battle of Valcour took place on October 11, 1776.

The War of 1812 brought forth the Peru militia who fired the first shots in the victorious and decisive Battle of Plattsburgh in September 1814. The opening of Plattsburgh Air Force Base in 1955 brought thousands of military personnel to the area. The majority resided within the Peru Central School District, which grew from 800 students to over 3,000.

The present population of Peru is 6,999 according to the 2010 census. Long gone are most of the timber and iron related industries and the many mills that once lined the banks of Peru's rivers. Fires have taken their toll on many buildings in the center of the village. It is now a relatively quiet semi-rural residential area surrounded by thousands of acres of apple orchards and dairy farms.

PLACES OF INTEREST

Babbie Farm and Learning Museum has a collection of farm equipment from years past on display. Open May thru October. Friday-Sunday, 10 am – 4 pm. 250 River Rd., Peru.

Purchase produce at Rulfs' Orchard & Roadside Shop and 'pick yourself' strawberries and blueberries. It's a great family outing. 531 Bear Swamp Rd., Peru.

AuSable Point State Park on Lake Champlain has beachfront and camping areas. A boat ramp at Valcour gives boaters easy access to Lake Champlain and Valcour Island, which is 895 total acres owned by NYS. There are also seven miles of trails on the densely wooded island and camping is allowed by permit only. The island is mostly in Town of Peru and part in Plattsburgh. www.historiclakes.org/valcour/valcour_island.htm

Material courtesy of Peter Glushko, Supervisor Town of Peru

DATE: _____ WEATHER: _____

MEMORIES: _____

_____

_____

_____

_____

_____

_____

_____

_____

_____

_____

_____

_____

_____

_____

[Passport Stamp / Signature Here]

Visitors to the Babbie Farm and Learning Museum learn about New York's rural and farm life development from seeing horse drawn implements, gas engines, early tractors and other supporting tools in action. There are demonstrations for visitors of all ages - some of which are interactive. Peter Glushko

165

PLATTSBURGH

The Town of Plattsburgh is in eastern Clinton County, near the NW shore of Lake Champlain in part of the northeastern Adirondacks.

The territory around what we know as Plattsburgh was occupied largely by the Iroquois, Western Abenaki, Mohican, and Mohawk people prior to the time the first recorded European sailed into the Champlain Valley. Samuel de Champlain claimed the region as part of New France in 1609.

No permanent settlement was made while French and English fur traders and native peoples vied for dominance in the area. Conflicts led to the French and Indian War until 1763 when the French relinquished control of the region to the English.

The conclusion of hostilities gave William Gilliland and Count Charles De Fredenburgh, a former Captain in the British Army, an opportunity to explore the richness of the area that was to become Plattsburgh. Gilliland built his Possession House near the Salmon River at the southern end of the present Town in 1766. De Fredenburgh built a stately family home and mill on the Saranac River and workers' cabins near the Lake in 1770. In 1775, tensions leading up to the American Revolution forced De Fredenburgh, a Loyalist, to seek refuge for his family in Montreal. The Count returned to protect his property, but found it burned and he mysteriously disappeared.

It was safe enough by 1785 for Zephaniah Platt and 32 others to settle the area. The NYS Legislature granted Platt's company 33,000 acres along with the right to establish the first Township in what is now Clinton County. Most of the acreage came from lands claimed

by De Fredenburgh but that claim had been annulled by New York. The land encompassed a large geographic area including today's towns of Peru (1792), Beekmantown (1820), Saranac (1824), and Schuyler Falls (1828).

The Town's population grew during the 1950s due to the establishment of the Plattsburgh Air Force Base. Rapid expansion continued into the 1960s with the construction of the Adirondack Northway and Plattsburgh State University of NY, and continued during the 1970s and 1980s. The closure of Plattsburgh Air Force Base in 1995 led to the conversion of the base to civil development, housing, industry and business. With a population of 11,685 residents (1997 estimate) and growing, the Town benefits from a strong regional economy and is home to the Plattsburgh International Airport, educational institutions including Clinton Community College, and a growing number of significant businesses.

PLACES TO VISIT

Champlain Valley Transportation Museum. Includes artifacts and displays on the history of land and water transportation in the region. Features the Lozier Motor Company, an automobile manufacturing business during the early 1900s that built exquisite and expensive vehicles. 12 Museum Way, Plattsburgh.

Imaginarium Children's Museum. Features interactive exhibits based on math, science, art, music. www.imaginariumchildrensmuseum.org

Battle of Plattsburgh Museum. Exhibits and artifacts of the War of 1812 and the Battle of Plattsburgh. 31 Washington Rd., Plattsburgh. www.battleofplattsburgh.org

DATE: _____ WEATHER: _____

MEMORIES: _____

_____

_____

_____

_____

_____

_____

_____

_____

_____

[Passport Stamp / Signature Here]

Clinton County Historical Association Museum. 98 Ohio Avenue, Plattsburgh. www.clintoncountyhistorical.org

NYS Parks:
Point AuRoche. Beach, picnic facilities, boating. 19 Camp Red Cloud Rd.

Crab and Valcour Islands. Off the coast of Plattsburgh in Lake Champlain. Site of many American Revolution & War of 1812 battles.

Cumberland State Park. Developed during the 1930s by Civilian Conservation Corps Veterans. Beach, picnic area, and campground. 152 Cumberland Head Road, Plattsburgh.

The Saranac River passes through the Town on its way to Lake Champlain and provides fantastic vistas for paddling of all types. The Cadyville Beach (2145 Rt. 3) is the perfect place to drop in your boat and paddle or fish. Lake Champlain provides some of the best bass fishing in the state!

Cadyville Disc Golf Course. Take Rt. 3 towards Saranac, turn left onto Goddeau Rd. before the gas station. The course is roughly an eighth of a mile on the left at Cadyville Rec Park. www.townofplattsburghrecreation.com

Material courtesy of Melanie DeFayette, Plattsburgh Rec & Youth Services Director

Cumberland Bay State Park, on the northwestern shore of Lake Champlain, is a popular day use park with a natural sandy beach for swimming and relaxing. NYS Office of Parks, Recreation and Historic Preservation

SARANAC

The Town of Saranac is in SE Clinton County, west of Plattsburgh, and the northeastern corner of the Adirondacks. It is named after the Saranac River that flows through the town. The town's major road is Rt. 3.

Formed from the Town of Plattsburgh in 1824, the Town of Saranac developed along the Saranac River in Clinton Co. The original settlers depended on the river and the woods for their livelihood. As the town grew the settlements of Saranac Hollow, Picketts Corners, Redford, Standish, Riverview, and Clayburg sprang up.

From about 1830-1850 the Redford Crown Glass Works produced highly prized crown window glass that was used throughout the eastern United States. Even more desirable than the window glass, however, are the pieces produced by the talented Redford glass blowers. The Clinton County Historical Museum in Plattsburgh and the Alice T. Miner Museum in Chazy have exhibits of the witches balls, canes, pitchers, and other glass creations in the beautiful clear, aqua blue that identifies Redford Glass.

During the 1850s iron ore was discovered in the region and the area boomed. The residents used the surrounding forests to provide charcoal to keep the forge fires burning continuously. The farmers enlarged their fields and were able to offer their produce for the forge workers and their families. Although the forge fires along the Saranac had been extinguished by the 1890s, Standish grew as some of the best iron ore in the world was mined in nearby Lyon Mountain.

The Civil War played a big role in Saranac. Saranac was credited with enlisting more

soldiers per capita of any town in New York State. The soldiers and their families paid dearly as over 70 men died of disease, in battle, and in prison. Their names are listed on a white bronze monument in the Saranac Independence Cemetery.

RECREATION

Like the early citizens, we depend on the river today. The Saranac has some fabulous flat-water and level III-V whitewater canoeing and kayaking. You can always spot anglers trying for the big one in the river as well as in many of the brooks and streams.

The forests continue to provide Saranac with many opportunities. The New Land Trust offers well-marked hiking, snowshoeing, and Cross-country skiing trails. The Sable Highlands Conservation Easement allows public use of private lands for various forms of recreation.

POINTS OF INTEREST

Cemeteries: For those with a penchant for history, visits to the Saranac Independence Cemetery in Saranac, the Assumption of Mary Cemetery in Redford, and the St. Michael's Cemetery in Standish will provide a glimpse into the area's past. Redford and Saranac cemeteries are the final resting places for two of the five soldiers from Saranac who helped capture John Wilkes Booth. All three cemeteries show the migration of families to the area from Ireland, French Canada, Eastern Europe, and other areas.

Hill and Hollow Music: Check their schedule of music events. www.hillandhollowmusic.org

NYS Outdoor Activities: www.dec.ny.gov/62.html

DATE: _____ WEATHER: _____

MEMORIES: _____
_____
_____
_____
_____
_____
_____
_____
_____
_____
_____
_____
_____
_____

[Passport Stamp / Signature Here]

Town of Saranac: www.townofsaranac.com

New Land Trust in Saranac: Preserved land & trails. www.newlandtrust.org

Although the times have changed, the river and the land that formed Saranac continue to play a major role in its life.

Material courtesy of Jan Couture, Town of Saranac Historian

The Civil War Monument (erected 1888) in the Independence Cemetery on Rt. 3 in Saranac honors the Civil War soldiers from Saranac. Five men from the 16th NY aided in capturing John Wilkes Booth. Each side of the monument identifies a major Civil War Battle. The battles that the 419 soldiers participated in are also listed. Soldiers who died are listed and how they succumbed: 40 died from disease, 12 died in prison, and 19 were killed in battle. Jan Couture

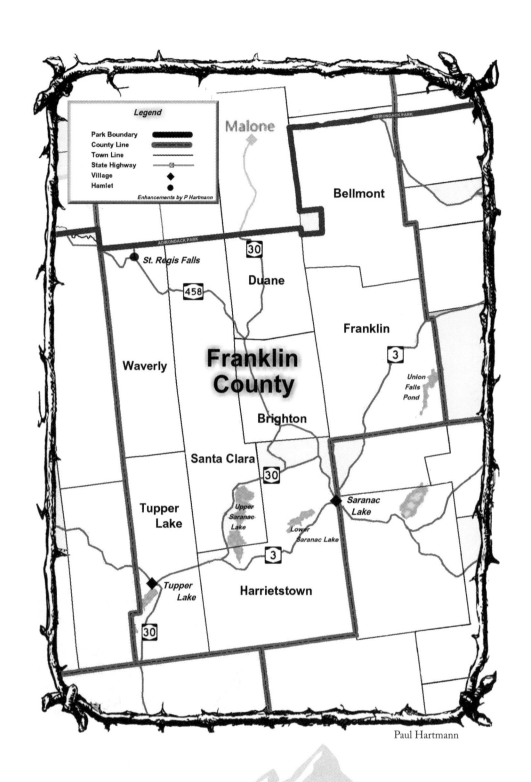

Legend

Park Boundary
County Line
Town Line
State Highway
Village
Hamlet

Enhancements by P Hartmann

Malone

Bellmont

ADIRONDACK PARK

St. Regis Falls

30

Duane

458

Franklin

3

Waverly

Franklin
County

Union
Falls
Pond

Brighton

Santa Clara

30

Upper
Saranac
Lake

Saranac
Lake

Tupper
Lake

Lower
Saranac Lake

3

Tupper
Lake

Harrietstown

30

Paul Hartmann

CHAPTER 6

REGION VI:
FRANKLIN COUNTY

BELLMONT

The Town of Bellmont is located in the northeast section of Franklin County and southeast of Malone in the northern Adirondack Mountains. The town includes these hamlets: Bellmont Center, Mountain View, Owls Head, Brainardsville, Bryants Mill, and Wolf Pond.

On March 16, 1833 the Town of Bellmont was created from the adjacent Town of Chateaugay. It included all of the territory now comprising the town of Franklin. The town's name in French, Bellemont, means beautiful mountain. The town was named for William Bell, of the city of New York, who had been an employee of William Constable. He is best remembered for his part in Macomb's Purchase, the giant real estate speculation which included about a tenth of NYS.

In 1838, a strip one mile wide along the north border of Bellmont was annexed from Chateaugay. Bellmont is mountainous and sparsely populated, with little territory suitable for sustained agriculture. Most of the lands are within Adirondack Park, a factor that inhibits economic development. However, dairy farms exist in the mile-wide strip on the north and in the land near Brainardsville.

There is a small section in Owls Head where during the 1800s and early 1900s crops of hops and potatoes were grown for markets in other parts of the state and overseas. Other industry included mining for iron ore, logging for charcoal production (used in iron ore smelting), and lumber. Most of the lumber production went to kilns and sawmills outside the township. The St. Lawrence and Adirondack Railroad, which ran through Mountain View and Owls Head, introduced travelers from downstate and Canada to the area.

POINTS OF INTEREST

The town has three significant lakes and many streams and ponds. Many second homes surround Lower Chateaugay Lake near Brainardsville and Indian Lake and Mountain View Lake. These and other smaller bodies of water, including the Salmon River and a stretch of the Chateaugay River, encourage year-round recreation. Both rivers and their headwater lakes provide great fishing. Extensive trails for snowmobiles and ATVs attract visitors from downstate New York, Quebec, Ontario, and nearby areas of New England. Second-home property taxes provide a significant portion of the town's budget.

There are many dairy farms and logging operations. The McCadam Cheese factory in nearby Chateaugay is an important customer for the dairy farmers. Some say the award-winning aged cheddar is the best in the nation. www.mccadam.coop

Many Bellmont residents are employed by Franklin County and the Central School in nearby Malone. Many residents travel as much as 100 miles round trip daily to jobs in Plattsburgh and Massena.

Volunteers operate the Fire Department in Owls Head, the food bank, and other essential services that knit the community together.

Material courtesy of Robert Hest, Resident of Bellmont

DATE: _____ WEATHER: _____

MEMORIES: _____

_____

_____

_____

_____

_____

_____

_____

_____

_____

_____

_____

_____

_____

_____

_____

_____

[Passport Stamp / Signature Here]

Sailing on Mountain View Lake in the hamlet of Mountain View near Rt. 27.
Robert Hest

BRIGHTON

The Town of Brighton is located 11 miles north of Saranac Lake Village on Rt. 86, north of Harrietstown. Rt. 30 crosses the west part of Brighton from south to north.

HISTORY

Brighton, est. in 1858, was composed mostly of family subsistence farms. Later 3 large farms were approved for potato seeding.

There were two TB sanatoriums, St. Gabriels (1897 to 1963) and Rainbow (1910 to 1934). Great camps were also built by wealthy visitors, and some of these families are still here. The resort business grew and many "sports" visited in small and large resorts. There was the Rainbow Inn on Rainbow Lake, and Paul Smith's Hotel on Lower St. Regis Lake, which became the famous Adirondack hotel hosting 500 people. The hotel property has become part of Paul Smith's College since the 1930s. Townspeople have built four churches; two of which are still in use. There used to be four schools, but now all students attend school in Saranac Lake. Population today is about 1,000, not counting the college students. Neighborhoods include Gabriels, Rainbow Lake, Paul Smiths, Keeses Mills, McColloms, Easy Street, and Split Rock Rd.

PLACES TO VISIT

White Pine Camp at 432 White Pine Rd. (off Rt. 86). This was the 1926 summer white house for President Calvin Coolidge. Located on Osgood Pond, it is now a restored resort with four-season lodging for the public. Tours are available Wednesday and Saturday, June thru the end of summer. 518-327-3030, www.whitepinecamp.com

Paul Smith's College. The Paul Smith's hotel property has become Paul Smith's College. The beautiful and interesting campus is on Lower St. Regis Lake. 7777 Rt. 30, Brighton. www.paulsmiths.edu

Paul Smith's College Visitor Interpretive Center. 3000 acres, 30 miles of hiking, cross-country skiing around lakes and rivers, nature interpretation, birding. Located off Rt. 30, north of the college entrance. 518-327-6241

Tucker Potato Farm. Over 100-year-old farm run by the same family. Tours, strawberry picking, veggies, and in late summer/fall there is a huge corn maze. Located on Hobart Rd., off Rt. 86. 518-637-1230

Moody's Christmas Store & Tree Farm, c. 1929. 'Cut your own' or just pick up your Christmas tree and live green decorations. Store open April until Christmas. Located on Co. Rt. 55, with an entrance off Rt. 86. 518-891-2468

Places to Hike and Ski:
St. Regis Mountain (in the Town of Santa Clara), trail access (in Brighton) off Keeses Mills Rd., Paul Smiths. St. Regis Mountain is one of Saranac Lake's "6ers Challenge" and the summit has a fire tower.

Paul Smith's College VIC trails. 1 mile north of Paul Smith's College on Rt. 30. Trail map at www.adirondackvic.org

Other trails are Jack Rabbit, Hays Brook, Red Dot, and Slush Pond.

Places to Canoe:
St. Regis Lakes: put in at Paul Smith's College; Black Lake-Long Lake: put in across from St. Regis Mt. Trail access road; Rainbow Lake: put in after short carry from Clark Wardner

174

DATE: _____ WEATHER: _____

MEMORIES: _____

_____

_____

_____

_____

_____

_____

_____

_____

_____

[Passport Stamp / Signature Here]

Rd.; Osgood Pond: put in off White Pine Rd.; Jones Pond: put in off Jones Pond. Rd. (Co. Rt. 31); Barnum Pond: put in off Rt. 30 north of Osgood Pond; Mountain Pond: put in off Rt. 30 north of Barnum Pond; Meecham Lake, put in off Rt. 30 at northern edge of Brighton.

Historic Sites:
Brighton Town Hall. 100 years old, built by Ben Muncil, builder of great camps. On the National Register of Historic Places and recently restored. Open Tuesday and Thursday afternoons. 12 Co. Rt. 31.
518-327-3202

St. Johns in the Wilderness Church is a 1929 stone church on Rt. 86 near Paul Smith's College.

Places to Eat:
St. Regis Café at Paul Smith's College is a student hospitality training restaurant with excellent food. Open to the public but reservations are required. Lunch is served Monday thru Friday, 10:30 am – 2 pm and a Dinner Banquet on Wednesday.
518-327-6355

Packbasket Diner at 881 Rt. 86, Gabriels.

The Shamrock Diner & Bar at 83 Co. Rt. 55, Gabriels.

Brighton Mini Mart offers a deli, groceries, and pizza. 846 Rt. 86, Gabriels.

Material courtesy of Pat Willis, Resident of Brighton

Shown above is the 1926 summer white house for President Calvin Coolidge. Located on Osgood Pond, it is now a restored resort with 4-season lodging for the public. Laurent Inard

175

DUANE

The Town of Duane is a quiet pristine town located in Franklin County in the northern Adirondack Park. It is approx. 18 miles south of Malone via Rt. 30 and 25 miles north of Saranac Lake.

Duane was formed from the Town of Malone Jan. 24, 1828, the first settlement in the town having been made about 1824 by men employed by James Duane, from whom the town takes its name. At that time it included Brighton and three townships of Harrietstown.

The Meacham Lake Hotel was a popular tourist resort until it closed in 1921. The land was purchased by New York State and converted to a campground by the Civilian Conservation Corps.

PLACES OF INTEREST

Meacham Lake State Park: Has a picnic area, beach, campground, and boat launch, hiking, cross-country skiing, snowshoeing and snowmobiling. Directions: From Lake Placid take Rt. 86 through Saranac Lake to Paul Smiths; turn right on Rt. 30N for approx. 9.5 miles. 119 State Camp Rd., Duane.

Deer River Campsites: Has fishing, boating, swimming, and family activities. 83 sites and 5 cabins available for rent (Co. Rt. 14) 123 Deer River Dr., Duane. 518-483-0060

Deer River Flow: Great fishing, kayaking, and canoeing. Access at Cold Brook Rd. off Rt. 30.

Debar & Debar Pond: Hiking, fishing, cross-country skiing, and snowshoeing. From Loon Lake Road of CR25 or can hike in via Meacham Lake State Park.

Pond and Bog Trail and Observation Area: 351 Co. Rt. 26, Malone. Take Rt. 30 to Duane, at the intersection of Rt. 30 and Rt. 26 then go east onto Co. Rt. 26 for 1 mile. Parking and trailhead on left.

Loon Lake fire tower: Trail and parking area. The trailhead is on the west side of Co. Rt. 26 in the Town of Franklin.

Have a picnic at Community Park! From Rt. 30 take Co. Rt. 26 to 1st left (Hogs back Rd.).

Wolf Pond Road Snowmobiling: South of Mountain View, near Co. Rt. 27. Follow power line section that goes N & S to great open and wooded sections. Trail information is avaliable in Mountain View.

There are many beautiful snowmobile trails in our town. You can enjoy a picnic or view an eagle's nest from Rt. 30. One can canoe or kayak on a variety of ponds, lakes or Deer River Flow.

For an interesting history of Duane, please visit www.duaneny.com.

Material courtesy of Sue Nitto, Town of Duane Clerk

DATE: _____ WEATHER: _____

MEMORIES: _____

_____

_____

_____

_____

_____

_____

_____

_____

_____

_____

_____

_____

_____

_____

_____

[Passport Stamp / Signature Here]

A bridge over Deer River Flow in Duane. Carol Murtagh & Paul Lemieux

FRANKLIN

The Town of Franklin consists of portions of Townships #9 and #10 of the Old Military Tract, and was formed on May 20, 1836 by being detached from the neighboring Town of Bellmont. It is in the southeast corner of Franklin County and is bordered on the north by the Town of Bellmont; on the west by Duane, Brighton, and a very small portion of Harrietstown; on its south by St. Armand in Essex County; and by Black Brook and Saranac in Clinton County on the east. It is composed of the hamlets of Vermontville and Onchiota.

Our town encompasses about 108,000 acres, or about 180 square miles. The landscape is of many broken and rolling hills, with some low mountains such as Loon Lake Mountain (our highest point, at 3,355 ft. and Kate Mountain. The land is heavily forested with a mix of both hardwood and softwood trees. Many small brooks, streams, and swamps weave through the area. Both branches of the Saranac River run through the town in a northeasterly direction towards Lake Champlain, while Hatch Brook and the Salmon River drain the extreme northern part of the town towards the St. Lawrence River. There are many small lakes and ponds such as Rainbow Lake, Kushaqua, Buck Pond, Loon Lake, and Franklin and Union Falls Flow.

The town's first settlement was at Franklin Falls on the Saranac River in 1827. Lumbering, farming, and a burgeoning hotel industry catering to sportsmen fueled a rapid growth of the area from the 1830s onward. Early settlers were mainly of Yankee, Irish, and French Canadian extract, and many current residents can trace their ancestry back to these pioneering families. The coming of the railroads in the 1880s saw the peak of

lumbering and farming. Fast forward to the present day and the town has maintained its rural character. It has only one true population center, Vermontville, which is the location of our town hall and highway department. While most residents work outside the town, it still maintains a tight-knit population of around 1,200 people.

INTERESTING PLACES TO VISIT

NYS DEC Buck Pond Campground in Onchiota: Camping, boating, swimming, biking, fishing, and hiking. 1339 Co. Rt. 60

The Six Nations Indian Museum: Open July & August. 1462 Co. Rt. 60, Onchiota

Kate Mountain Recreational Park: Children's playground, basketball courts, playing fields, and picnic pavilion. Rt. 3, Vermontville.

Norman Ridge in Vermontville: Sweeping views of Catamount, Kate, and Whiteface mountains, and the western High Peaks.

Snowmobiling on the old D & H Railroad Corridor, in the northern portion of the town.

There are 70 miles of town roads to travel; especially scenic in the fall.

Fishing and boating on many of the small lakes and ponds.

Hunting, hiking, and exploring on the large amount of the town's state lands.

Further details can be found on the town's website, www.townoffranklin.com.

Material courtesy of Kevin Ransom, Town of Franklin Historian

DATE: _____ WEATHER: _____

MEMORIES: _____

_____

_____

_____

_____

_____

_____

_____

_____

_____

_____

_____

_____

_____

_____

_____

[Passport Stamp / Signature Here]

A view of an old barn and Whiteface Mountain from Norman Ridge Road in
Vermontville. Loretta Ransom

HARRIETSTOWN & SARANAC LAKE VILLAGE

Harrietstown is in the southeast corner of Franklin County. Most of its population of 5,575, is concentrated in the village of Saranac Lake. It is composed of part of the Village of Saranac Lake and these hamlets: Axton Landing, Harrietstown, Lake Clear, Lake Clear Junction, McMasters Crossing, and Wawbeek. There are many lakes: Clear, Colby, Oseetah, and Upper, Middle, and Lower Saranac lakes.

HISTORY

Harrietstown began to be settled before 1812 by inhabitants of the adjoining counties. Harrietstown was formed from the Town of Duane in 1841. By the turn of the century, Saranac Lake had grown to become a health resort for those suffering from tuberculosis. The original Town Hall was built in Saranac Lake in 1888 and it burned on July 26, 1926. The current Town Hall was erected in 1928.

POINTS OF INTEREST

Harrietstown Town Hall is modeled after Independence Hall in Philadelphia. 39 Main St., Saranac Lake.

Adirondack Carousel is composed of 18 new handcarved figures of Adirondack wildlife and is located on Depot St., next to the Historic Railroad Station.

Adirondack Regional Airport is located approx. 5 miles NW of Saranac Lake. It accommodates small and large aircraft up to a Boeing 757. Cape Air has service to Boston. Each year nearly 10,000 passengers use private and commercial services at the airport.

Historic Locations:
Harrietstown Cemetery dates to its first burial in 1839. Take Rt. 86, 4 mi. north of Saranac Lake. The vista takes in the entire Whiteface Mountain Range.

Historic Railroad Stations in both Saranac Lake on Depot St., and in Lake Clear, I86, Lake Clear Jct.

Saranac Laboratory Museum features exhibits on local history, science, and patient care & is operated by Historic Saranac Lake. It is open year-round and located at 89 Church St. Saranac Lake.

Bartók Cabin is the humble cabin where the great Hungarian composer Béla Bartok spent the last summer of his life (1945) and where he composed some of his greatest work. To visit, contact Historic Saranac Lake.

Stevenson Cottage. Author Robert Louis Stevenson came to Saranac Lake for his health in 1887 and stayed in this cottage. It holds the largest collection of Stevenson memorabilia in the world. 11 Stevenson Lane, Saranac Lake.

Recreation:
Dewey Mountain is owned and operated by the Town of Harrietstown, and provides lighted trails for cross-country skiing, snowshoeing, hiking, and mountain bike trails that are used year round by all ages from the very young to seniors. The facility was the starting place for many of the Olympic athletes in both the 2010 and 2014 Winter Olympics. The Olympic athletes include Tim Burke, Annelies Cook, and 2010 Men's Nordic Combined Gold Medalist, Bill Demong. A new lodge will be constructed in 2014.

DATE: _____ WEATHER: _____

MEMORIES: _____

_____

_____

_____

_____

_____

_____

_____

_____

_____

_____

_____

_____

_____

[Passport Stamp / Signature Here]

Latour Park: Picnic area on Lake Colby, Rt. 86 across from the Adirondack Medical Center.

Waterways:
Within the boundaries of Harrietstown there are 118 public and private bodies of water, rivers, and streams. Many of these have access for motorized boats, canoe, and kayak use. These waterways include the Northern Forest Canoe Trail. Waterway events include the internationally recognized Round the Mountain Canoe and Kayak Classic, summer and winter fishing derbies.

Material courtesy of Mary Hotaling, Town of Harrietstown Historian & Councilman Ronald Keough

Saranac Lake was a renowned health resort specializing in the treatment of tuberculosis. In order to break winter's chill and to promote outdoor sports and games, the Pontiac Club was formed in November 1896. The following year they sponsored a one-day fancy dress winter carnival in 1897. Then in 1898 it was called the Pontiac Club Carnival. Today it is the longest-running event of its kind in the eastern U.S. The Carnival has expanded to a 10-day festival that includes two parades, sports, performances, and three sets of spectacular fireworks. Mary Hotaling

181

SANTA CLARA

The Town of Santa Clara is in southwestern Franklin County and in the northern Adirondack Park. It is a narrow strip of land starting in the south from Middle and Upper Saranac lakes to the Town of Brandon in the north. It consists of these hamlets: Saranac Inn, Santa Clara, Bay Pond, Floodwood, Derrick, Madawaska, Kildare, and Spring Cove. The population was 395 at the 2000 census.

Santa Clara includes these lakes: Middle Saranac, Madawaska Pond, and Weller Pond and the 58 ponds of the Saint Regis Canoe Area, presently the only Canoe Wilderness Area in the park, as well as most of 4,700-acre Upper Saranac Lake.

HISTORY

In 1888 the town of Santa Clara was formed from the Town of Brandon. An addition from Brandon was added to Santa Clara in 1896. Logging was an important occupation. The name Santa Clara is derived from the wife of early town businessman, John Hurd who operated the Northern Adirondack Railroad from Moira to Santa Clara and then to Tupper Lake. Hurd built the railroad to transport logs to the north. It eventually failed.

Millionaire oil man, William Rockefeller, began buying property in the town around 1896 to establish an estate at Bay Pond, that was used by members of his family during the summer. Brandon, a community located north of Bay Pond, became part of the Rockefeller estate and its buildings were removed. His estate totaled approx. 53,000 acres. Locals had many disputes with Rockefeller.

Today tourism and recreation are the most important economy of the town.

RECREATION

Fishing:
Santa Clara is rated among the top fishing waters in Franklin County for trout and pike.

Saint Regis Canoe Area: A 19,000-acre wilderness area with 58 ponds (no motorized vehicles are allowed). It's a pond-hopper's paradise. Many carries are short and most kayak and canoe routes can be done as an unencumbered day trip. It attracts canoeists and kayakers from across the country.
In addition, the area provides excellent opportunities for hiking, camping, cross-country skiing, hunting, comma and fishing.

Hiking:
St. Regis Mt. fire tower: This 35' tower was constructed in 1918 and the (2,882') summit provides a panoramic view of the St. Regis Canoe Area. The tower will be restored in the future. Directions: intersection of Rts. 86 and 30 in front of Paul Smith's College, drive north on Rt. 30 for about 200 yds. and turn left on Keese Mills Rd. Follow this road for 2.5 miles and on the left is the DEC parking area. Walk on Topridge road, which was the road to the former estate of Marjorie Merriweather Post. Look on the right for the trailhead.

Camping:
Fish Creek State Campground: 322 campsites. It is considered by many as the finest & most attractive of all the Adirondack campgrounds. There is a natural sand shoreline and water access for most campsites. Both motorized and non-motorized boats are permitted.
An Interpretive Activity Program for adults and children. Canoeing, fishing, hiking, and bicycling are popular. 4523 Rt. 30, Saranac Lake. www.fishcreekpond.com

DATE: _____ WEATHER: _____

MEMORIES: _____

_____

_____

_____

_____

_____

_____

_____

_____

_____

_____

_____

_____

_____

_____

[Passport Stamp / Signature Here]

Rollins Pond State Campground: 442-acre pond. There are on-and-off water campsites. Canoes, rowboats, and kayaks are available for rent at the boat launch livery site. Great fishing for trout. Hiking, bicycling, and picnicking are other activities. 4523 Rt. 30, Saranac Lake.

Food & Supplies:
Knapp's Trading Post offers groceries, sandwiches, pizza, ice cream, camping supplies newspapers, and books. Located across from Fish Creek Campground.

Visit www.townofsantaclara.com for more.

Material courtesy of Roy Rosenbarker, Town of Santa Clara Historian

Fish Creek State Park has 355 sites accommodating all equipment from tents to 40-foot RV's with a natural sand shoreline and water access for most campsites. The sites are well treed with balsam fir, white pines, maple and birch trees dominating on sandy soil. Dave McGrath

183

ST. ARMAND

The Town of St. Armand is in the northwestern corner of Essex County north of Saranac Lake and Lake Placid. The town contains the northeastern part of Saranac Lake and these hamlets: Bloomingdale, Franklin Falls, and Trudeau. The Town of St. Armand encompasses 56.5 square miles and includes a northern part of the Village of Saranac Lake and part of Lake Placid.

The town was first settled in 1829 in the area currently known as Franklin Falls which was known as McLenathon Falls. The town was set off from the Town of Wilmington in 1844. In 1851 there was an area that was established with a post office, hotel with a stagecoach stop, a school, and many new homes. The hamlet of Bloomingdale had been established in the late 1840s and was officially named Bloomingdale in 1852 by local citizens.

Timber was the biggest commercial enterprise at that time, and C.P. Norton owned much of the land. In 1912 Paul Smith built a hydroelectric plant at Franklin Falls. This plant remains in place today, and is currently used as a relay station.

Trudeau Sanatorium was a facility established by Dr. Trudeau to cure patients of tuberculosis. It was purchased in 1884 for $400.00. Many of the original structures still stand on the property. It now houses the American Management Association and is in the northern part of the Village of Saranac Lake.

The first school was built in 1840 and the first teacher wasHarriet Hayes. The current school, Bloomingdale Elementary (kindergarten through fifth grade), is a bright and beautiful addition to the town. The playground is a popular spot for games and sliding.

Between 1861 and 1898, St. Armand had many volunteers for the Civil and Spanish Wars, sending the most volunteers per capita in all of Essex County. Captain James Pierce was one of these volunteers, and he was Supervisor for the Town of St. Armand for many years.

By 1906, Bloomingdale was a growing village, with many stores, hotels, and homes. In 1914 many men volunteered to fight in World War I. Following this war, many new settlers came to this area and Bloomingdale continued to grow and prosper.

During the 1930s, Rt. 3 was built as well as infrastructure and a wastewater treatment plant.

During the 1950s many businesses were sold or closed, and Bloomingdale became a more residential area. St. Armand has become more of a bedroom community for the larger towns of Saranac Lake, Lake Placid, Plattsburgh, and Malone.

Bloomingdale continues to accommodate several businesses, including Norman's Store (1699 Rt. 3), River Road Bait & Tackle (12 River Rd.), the Bloomin' Market (1719 Rt. 3), Specialty Wood Products (14 Mill St.), Teddy's Ice Cream (1663 Rt. 3), and The Four Corner's Diner (1692 Rt. 3), just to mention a few.

There is a wayside exhibit entitled "Patriots of St. Armand" in Veterans Memorial Park adjacent to the Town Hall.

The Town Hall has a library section made possible by the Saranac Lake Free Library. Stop by during business hours to borrow a book or two.

The beauty of St. Armand is boundless. Great

DATE: _____ WEATHER: _____

MEMORIES: _____

_____

_____

_____

_____

_____

_____

_____

_____

_____

_____

_____

_____

_____

_____

[Passport Stamp / Signature Here]

locations to visit for hiking, boating, hunting and fishing include Moose Pond, River Road, Bloomingdale Bog Trail, and Franklin Falls.

Please visit www.townofstarmand.com for more information.

Material courtesy of Davina M. Thurston, St. Armand Town Clerk

St. Armand Town Hall on Rt. 3 in Bloomingdale with a rainbow overhead. Davina M. Thurston

185

TUPPER LAKE TOWN & VILLAGE

The Town of Altamont, changed to the Town of Tupper Lake on July 16, 2004, is in the southwest corner of Franklin County. It includes the Village of Tupper Lake and these hamlets: Moody, Litchfield Park, Derrick, and Kildare. The town population was 5,971 in the 2010 census.

HISTORY

Tupper Lake had no official status as a town or village prior to 1890. The early village was composed of two parts, Tupper Lake proper and Faust. The town for a time held the distinction as the top lumber producer in New York State.

The village takes its name from a nearby lake, which, in turn, is the name of a surveyor, Ansel Norton Tupper, who drowned there while fishing in Tupper Lake.

The great fire of 1899 burned more than 169 structures in the village, two-thirds of them homes. The modern village grew out of this destruction and added all the amenities of a modern community earlier than many other villages in the state. Tupper Lake had its own department store and synagogue, and its sprawling railway yards, driven by the lumber trade, made it a hub for the surrounding Adirondack communities.

When the Oval Wooden Dish Co. (OWD) came to a stagnant economy in Tupper Lake in 1916, it brought prosperity with it. OWD, so called because of the oval wood dishes they produced by folding & stapling wood veneer, purchased about 75,000 acres of timber and built a huge sawmill and factory in Tupper Lake. The plant was the largest in Franklin Co. employing some 500 people. OWD made

millions of wooden bowls, dishes, spoons, forks, ice cream sticks & flat spoons used throughout the world. During the 1950s they added flooring, bowling pins, tongue depressors & furniture products. It closed its doors in 1964 leaving the huge smokestack that still marks the factory site.

In the 1940s the Village of Faust combined with the Village of Tupper Lake. The former Village of Faust was called "The Junction" due to the junction of railroad lines located in Faust.

The town sits on the shore of nine-mile long Tupper Lake that has a distinct history of pioneers, loggers, and Adirondack guides. The railway arrived in Tupper in the 1890s and much of the modern town was built in the boom years that followed. Tupper was the lumber capital of New York in the early 1900s. You can see the huge site of the giant mill that burned in a spectacular fire down on the lake shore. Today the site is a public park, and home to local events, including the annual Woodsmen Field Days festival where lumberjack skills are on display every July.

Tupper Lake still has a mixture of businesses, including lumbering, and it gives the town a distinct flavor. Tupper is a North-woods neighborhood, with a dash of Quebecois influence from its lumberjack heritage. There's even a part of town that locals call the French Village. If you're looking for a place with small town friendliness where neighbor watches out for neighbor, this is it.

POINTS OF INTEREST

The Wild Center, a nature museum, has walking trails, naturalist guides, movies,

DATE: _____ WEATHER: _____

MEMORIES: _____

_____

_____

_____

_____

_____

_____

_____

_____

_____

[Passport Stamp / Signature Here]

live exhibits including otters and 900 other animals. open daily except for holidays. 45 Museum Dr., Tupper Lake. 518-359-7800, www.wildcenter.org

Tupper Lake Heritage Museum is open July 1st to Labor Day. Weekdays from 11 am – 4 pm, weekends by appointment. 54 Pine Street Tupper Lake. 518-359-3676

Beth Joseph Synagogue, built in 1905, is the oldest synagogue in the Adirondacks. Open to the public, July and August. Tours: Tuesday thru Friday, 11 am – 3 pm. Lake St. (Rt.3), Tupper Lake.

Goff-Nelson Memorial Library. 41 Lake St., Tupper Lake.

Little Wolf Beach and Campground on Little Wolf Pond Rd. has 52 campsites, a picnic area and beach.

Woodsmen Field Days. This festival is an exciting annual event that attracts thousands of spectators and hundreds of competitors for a weekend of parades, logging demonstrations, competition, and fun. Visit tupper-lake.com.

Tupper Lake Municipal Park, on shore of Raquette Pond, has facilities for tennis, basketball, skateboard park, walking, and boating. Access from Demars Boulevard.

Material courtesy of Jon Kopp, Town of Tupper Lake Historian

The Wild Center, a nature museum on 45 Museum Dr., has walking trails, naturalist guides, bookstore, movies, and live exhibits including otters and 900 other animals. Jon Kopp

187

WAVERLY

The Town of Waverly is in the western part of Franklin County southwest of the City of Malone. The town contains the hamlet of St. Regis Falls and Dexter Lake.

What does a little town like Waverly, or the quaint Village of St. Regis Falls (pop. 1,010) have to offer visitors on a trek through the Adirondacks? Not a lot of excitement, for sure, but a village of friendly folks, an outstanding campsite, two restaurants, one quick-stop, a public Reading Center (18 North Main), three churches, an expert rescue squad, and a small log museum full of history about this once booming lumber town. St. Regis Falls is located at the intersection of Rts. 458, 14 & 5.

Our town campsite is located along the St. Regis River and has picturesque waterfalls that are a treat to see as mists send out a rainbow of colors on a sunny day. The campsite has full hook-ups as well as tenting sites. Several employees make sure your stay is safe and enjoyable. At the entrance to the campsite is a small Log History Museum, open on weekends or by appointment. The museum contains interesting items from early town businesses and logging camps. If you are a native of the area, you will be interested in the hundreds of pictures from early school days and picture postcards of early factories, etc. Leroux Lodge Quickstop (14 Spring St., St. Regis Falls) has fuel, food, and groceries for your camping needs.

There are two good small restaurants and a quick-stop in the town. The local reading center offers access to a computer and welcomes campers to borrow books. There is a very nice restaurant, Deer Valley Trails, located about six miles outside of St. Regis Falls that has excellent food and a wooded Adirondack view that attracts diners from miles away. They have new and lovely cabins to rent at a reasonable price. In winter, snowmobiles are popular at this restaurant. Deer often look through the windows at diners. Deer Valley Trails is about one mile from Azure Mountain, which offers a well-groomed trail to the summit with wonderful views and a restored fire tower. The three local churches have regular services each week.

Azure Mt. fire tower: Each year thousands of people climb Azure Mountain to visit the restored 1918 fire tower. During the summer and fall volunteer guides tell the history of the tower and point out the surrounding mountains and the plants & animals of the region. The Azure Mountain Friends serve as guides and stewards, and maintain the tower & trail. From St. Regis Falls go SE on Rt. 458 to Azure Mt. Rd. Then drive 7 miles to trailhead parking on the right. www.azuremountain.org

Whether you are riding your bike, hauling a camper, or driving your car or snowmobiles, come our way. We love company.

Material courtesy of Judy Wever,
Town of St. Regis Falls Historian

188

DATE: _____ WEATHER: _____

MEMORIES: _____

_____

_____

_____

_____

_____

_____

_____

_____

_____

_____

_____

_____

_____

[Passport Stamp / Signature Here]

Azure Mountain fire tower is a restored 1918 tower that attracts thousands of hikers year round. The Azure Mountain Friends serve as guides and stewards, and maintain the tower and trail. During the summer and fall volunteer guides tell the history of the tower and point out the surrounding mountains and the plants and animals of the region. Dave Petrelli

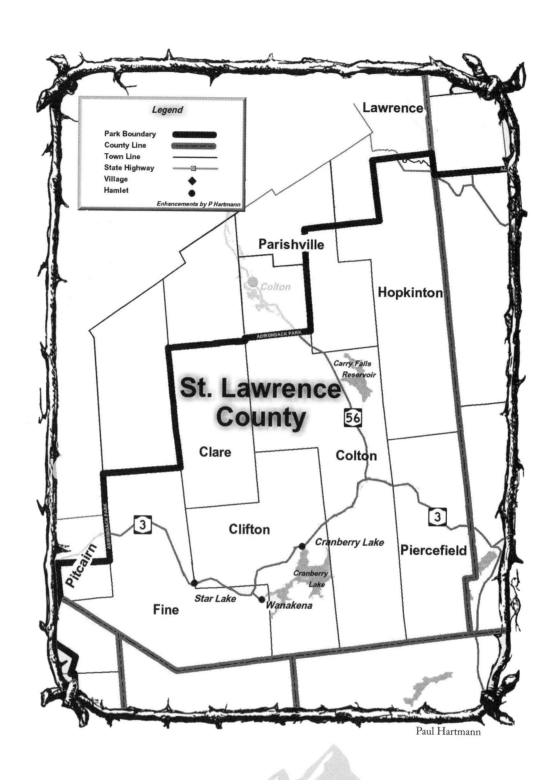

Legend

Park Boundary	
County Line	
Town Line	
State Highway	
Village	◆
Hamlet	●

Enhancements by P Hartmann

Lawrence

Parishville

Colton

Hopkinton

St. Lawrence County

Carry Falls Reservoir

56

Clare

Colton

3

Clifton

Cranberry Lake

Piercefield

Cranberry Lake

Pitcairn

3

Star Lake

Wanakena

Fine

Paul Hartmann

CHAPTER 7

REGION VII:

ST. LAWRENCE COUNTY

191

CLARE

The Town of Clare, in south central St. Lawrence County, is south of Canton and includes the hamlets of Clare and New Bridge. It was formed from part of the towns of Pierrepont and Clifton and comprises 29,695 acres. It officially became a town in December 1880 and was the last town formed in the county. In 2010 its population was 105.

Clare, named for a county in Ireland, was a busy community in the last half of the 19th Century. It had a blacksmith shop, cheese factory, church, hotel across the river from church, post office near the center of town, a tavern, a barrel or stave factory down at Lampson Falls, and many thriving farms. There were four schools: Upper School of Colton Dist. #1, Lower School or Dewey, Dist. #2, the Clare Mill Dist. #3 school, and White, Dist. #4 school on the White Rd. Town meetings were held in the Dewey School until February 1897, when the town voted to raise $600 to build a Town Hall on 1/2 acre purchased from John Bird for $10. The first recorded Town Board meeting in the new building was Feb. 1, 1897.

In 1886 Clarksboro, near Twin Falls, was settled as a mining town for the Clifton Mining Co., which was incorporated as Clifton Iron Co. In 1864 Myers Steel & Wire Co. operated a blast furnace to manufacture steel from their iron ore mines. A railroad was started in 1866 to run to East DeKalb. The railroad was made completely of wood except for strap iron nailed to the maple rails. Two miles east of the hamlet the Dannemora Steel Mines started but abandoned its mine. In 1941 Hanna Coal & Ore Co. operated the abandoned Dannemora Mine until December 1951. Clarksboro no longer exists.

New Bridge, about 4 miles above the hamlet of Clare, was a lumbering settlement with 50 families. It began in 1906 when Milo Woodcock of Edwards brought in a portable sawmill. The mill grew to become one of the largest around with an output of 3-4 thousand feet of lumber a day.

POINTS OF INTEREST

Honor Roll for our war veterans in front of the Clare Museum.

Town of Clare Museum: The old Town Hall, built in 1897, was converted in 1968 to a museum and is now listed on the State & National Register of Historic Places. The Museum is open by appointment by calling 315-386-3849. It is closed during the winter. During August "Clare Day" is held and the Museum is open from 9 am until the celebration ends. A covered dish lunch is held and families gather in the Town Building across the road from the Museum.

Lampson Falls is popular for swimming with local residents and college students. The trailhead is just north of an airstrip which is north of the hamlet of Degrasse in the Town of Russell. Directions from Canton: Drive on Park St. past St. Lawrence University and follow Co. Rt. 27 to the town of Clare. After crossing into the town of Clare, look for a sign on your right. Directions from Rt. 3 just east of Fine: Take Co. Rt. 27. The road will make a righthand turn on to Cracker Box Rd. that is still Co. Rt. 27. After a few miles there will be a "T" where Co. Rt. 17 & Co. Rt. 27 intersect. Turn right in the hamlet of Degrasse. Then go 4.6 miles to the trailhead. www.nnywaterfalls.com/grasseriver/lampsonsfalls/

192

DATE: _____ WEATHER: _____

MEMORIES: _____

_____

_____

_____

_____

_____

_____

_____

_____

_____

_____

_____

_____

_____

_____

[Passport Stamp / Signature Here]

Harper Falls: A very picturesque falls with a slide not far from Lampson Falls. Directions: Go to the intersection of Co. Rt. 17 & Co. Rt. 27 in the hamlet of Degrasse. Go NE on Co. Rt. 27 for 7.4 miles. Then go left on the Downerville Rd. and go past the Clare town barn. The trailhead is 0.5 mile down this road.

Material courtesy of Charlotte & Allen Peabody, Town of Clare Historians

The Town of Clare Museum is located in the old 1897 Town Hall. In August "Clare Day" is held and the Museum is open from 9 am until the celebration ends. Charlotte Peabody

CLIFTON

The Town of Clifton, in the NW section of the Adirondacks and the southern part of St. Lawrence County, is approx. 25 miles west of Tupper Lake on Rt. 3. It contains the following hamlets: Cranberry Lake, Newton Falls, Windfall, and part of Star Lake.

In 1868 the town was formed from the Town of Pierrepont. The town held its first town meeting in the school house of the Clifton Iron Mine Company. Mining resumed in the late 19th Century at Benson Mines, and continued sporadically through the 1970s.

When you enter the hamlet of Cranberry Lake from the east or west on Rt. 3, the welcoming sign says "Forever Wild," which is aptly applied to the Town of Clifton. The predominant geographical feature of the Town is Cranberry Lake. Originally much smaller, Cranberry Lake about doubled in size after the 1867 erection of a dam on the Oswegatchie River at the lake's outlet to become what was once the largest lake inside the Blue Line. Nearly all of Cranberry Lake lies within the Town of Clifton. Lumbering was the main occupation of the area in the late 1800s and early 1900s.

POINTS OF INTEREST

Cranberry Lake State Campground: The DEC maintains a well-equipped campground on the east shore at the end of Lone Pine Rd. In addition, there are 46 remote boat-access-only campsites spread out around the lake. It has 173 campsites; hot showers, picnic area, beach, boating, fishing, and hiking trails. 243 Lone Pine Rd., Cranberry Lake.

Recreation:
Brook trout and smallmouth bass both thrive in Cranberry Lake, with brookies averaging

12-16". Non-native pike in excess of 15 pounds have also been caught here. In addition to fishing (both ice and water), camping and hiking, other popular activities include boating, four-wheeling, snowmobiling and cross-country skiing.

Hiking:
Numerous hiking trails fan out in all directions, with some trailheads requiring a boat to reach them. The new "Cranberry Lake 50" is a trail that circumnavigates the lake in 50 miles, and has become a 'destination hike.' Favorite hikes include those to Bear Mountain, Cat Mountain, and Sliding Rock Falls. Approx. two miles west of Cranberry Lake Village on Rt. 3 is the Peavine Swamp Ski Trail, which hikers use to see large, old-growth trees.

The vast majority of the Cranberry Lake shoreline is undeveloped. The Cranberry Lake Wild Forest and the Five Ponds Wilderness Area represent one of the largest unspoiled forests in the entire Northeast, encompassing thousands of acres.

A very pleasant drive on Tooley Pond Rd., which is to the west of Rt. 3 just below the dam, will take you to a small settlement called The Windfall, named after an 1845 windstorm that blew down a swath of trees a mile wide for several miles. This legendary cyclone started in Upper Canada and extended for almost 200 miles to Lake Champlain. If you continue through The Windfall on the same road, you will encounter several picturesque waterfalls just outside the Town of Clifton.

Material courtesy of Mark Friden, Town of Clifton Historian

DATE: _____ WEATHER: _____

MEMORIES: _____
_____
_____
_____
_____
_____
_____
_____
_____
_____
_____
_____
_____
_____
_____
_____

[Passport Stamp / Signature Here]

A view from Bear Mt. of Arnolds Point and Dead Creek Flow shows the vast
amount of undeveloped shoreline of Cranberry Lake. Mark Friden

COLTON

The Town of Colton, located south of Potsdam on Rt. 56, was formed from the Town of Parishville on April 12, 1843. Colton was the 27th town of St. Lawrence County created by the State Legislature. Colton was well known for its lumbering years, which started with a large gang mill being built in 1850. The lumbering business ceased in the early part of the 1900s.

The town itself witnessed the growth of hydro power beginning in the early 1950s. An area known as "Hollywood" was flooded.

The Town of Colton is home to "Sunday Rock," a towering glacial boulder weighing 35 tons which was once used as a landmark on the way to the South Woods. A preservation group was formed to save the rock during one of the many road widening projects. The rock was saved and put on donated land. Sunday Rock is now on the state and federal historic registers.

Colton has been known as a recreational destination because of the Raquette River. During the summer and early fall, water is released from the Colton Dam, making it a perfect place to hold white-water events. The river is also used for fishing, canoeing, kayaking, and swimming. There is also the Stone Valley Nature Trail, The John Stone Memorial Trail, and Higley Flow State Park located in Colton.

Sites of Interest

Colton Historical Museum. It usually opens from Memorial Day weekend until October 1st. 94 Main St., Colton.

Colton Hepburn Library. This beautiful library just celebrated its 100th Anniversary and is on the National Historic Register. 84 Main St., Colton. www.coltonhepburnlibrary.org

Sunday Rock Historic Site. Rt. 56, South Colton.

Zion Episcopal Church. It was built of the famous Potsdam sandstone in 1883 by the Clarkson family of Potsdam. 9 Main St., Colton.

Higley Flow State Park. The park is nestled among the Adirondack foothills on the picturesque Raquette River. It contains campsites, a sandy beach, canoeing and fishing, and hiking trails. The trails double as cross-country ski trails in winter, when snowmobiling, snowshoeing, and ice fishing are also allowed. 442 Coldbrook Drive, Colton. www.nysparks.com/parks/58/details.aspx

Stone Valley Trail. The 7.8 mile loop trail is on property owned by Brookfield Power. It is open year-round, but best from Spring through Fall. Trailhead directions: At the intersection of Main St. in Colton, proceed northeast. There are two parking areas. The first is on the left just before crossing the bridge. For the second, which is the preferred route for waterfalls, take the left after crossing the bridge. There is a lot immediately behind the fire hall but you want the lot past that.

For more information, visit the town's website at www.townofcolton.com.

Material courtesy of Dennis E. Eickhoff, Town of Colton Historian

DATE: _____ WEATHER: _____

MEMORIES: _____

_____

_____

_____

_____

_____

_____

_____

_____

_____

_____

_____

_____

_____

_____

_____

[Passport Stamp / Signature Here]

The Zion Episcopal Church was built of the famous Potsdam sandstone in 1883
by the Clarkson family of Potsdam. Dennis Eickhoff

FINE

The Town of Fine is located in southern St. Lawrence County in the northwest foothills of the Adirondack Mountains. It includes these hamlets: Fine, Wanakena, Star Lake, and Oswegatchie.

The Town of Fine, named after Judge John Fine who was involved in settling the town, was established in 1844 and lumbering was the chief occupation.

The town encompasses 169.4 square miles and the 2010 census population was 1,512.

The town is rich with natural resources and scenic beauty. Pristine Adirondack waterways are abundant in our lakes and rivers. We offer a fantastic opportunity to experience outdoor activities that include golfing, snowmobiling, ATV's, hunting, boating, canoeing, hiking, biking, cross-country skiing, and ice skating.

POINTS OF INTEREST

Adirondack Exhibit Center. 4195 Rt. 3, Star Lake.

Cathedral Rock fire tower. 257 Ranger School Rd., Wanakena.

Clifton-Fine Golf Course. A 9-hole municipal course with golf cart rentals, pro-shop, food, and tournaments. 4173 Rt.3, Star Lake. 315-848-3570, www.afineadirondacktown.org

SUNY ES&F Ranger School. Established in 1912, on the East Branch of the Oswegatchie River near Wanakena, it offers A.A.S. degrees in forest and natural resources management. 257 Ranger School Rd., Wanakena.

Pine Cone Grill. Ranger School Rd., Wanakena.

The Big Pine, a trail at the end of South Sore Rd. leads to one of the oldest white pine trees in the Adirondacks.

Wanakena Walking Tour. There are brochures avaliable at the kiosk at 6 Hamele St. www.wanakena.webs.com

Wanakena General Store. Groceries, gifts, books, camping goods, and 'Good Advice'. 315-848-3008

Packbasket Adventures. This B&B offers old-fashioned lodge and guide services. South Shore Rd. 315-848-3488, www.packbasketadventures.com

Historic Sites:
Fine Town Hall. 91 Rt. 58, Fine.

Wanakena Foot Bridge. Historic pedestrian suspension bridge constructed in 1902 that spans the Oswegatchie River. It was originally constructed to provide a crossing for the employees of the Rich Lumber Company. 38 River St. Wanakena.

Hiking/Canoe Locations:
Cranberry Lake. There is a 50-mile trail around the lake. www.cranberrylake50.org

Enjoy fishing and boating at the Oswegatchie River, Little River, and Star Lake.

Check out "Ten Favorite Hikes in the Townships of Clifton & Fine" an Adirondack Council brochure. Avaliable at www.townoffine.org.

The Town of Fine Municipal Office Building is located at 4078 Rt.3, Star Lake. Visit our website at www.townoffine.org.

Material courtesy of Mark Hall,
Town of Fine Supervisor

DATE: _____ WEATHER: _____

MEMORIES: _____
_____
_____
_____
_____
_____
_____
_____
_____
_____
_____
_____
_____
_____
_____

[Passport Stamp / Signature Here]

The Wanakena Foot Bridge is a historic pedestrian suspension bridge constructed in 1902. It's purpose was to provide a crossing for the employees of the Rich Lumber Company across the Oswegatchie River. Mark Hall

HOPKINTON

The Town of Hopkinton is located on Rt. 11B, 14 miles east from Potsdam and 25 miles west from Malone in St. Lawrence County. It is composed of these hamlets: Hopkinton, Catherineville, Nicholville, and Fort Jackson.

HISTORY

The Town was founded in 1802 by Col. Roswell Hopkins. It is the second largest town in St. Lawrence County.

Our Village Green (1808), Town Hall (1870), and Congregation Church (1892) were placed on the New York Register of Historic Places in 2013. There are picnic tables for public use on the Green. Farming and logging were the principal occupations and still are today.

For genealogists, we have three cemeteries that are well documented and many genealogies are on file in the historian's office.

POINTS OF INTEREST

Hopkinton Historical Museum is located on the west side of the Village Green. All three of these buildings can be shown to the public by appointment with the Historical Group. 7 Church St. www.townofhopkinton.com

Self-guided driving tour book of historic homes is free at the Town office and the historian's office. 2893 State Highway 11B in the village of Hopkinton. 315-328-4681

Sharlow's Camping Trailer site opened in the spring of 2014 on the Lake Ozonia Rd. It has showers, sewer disposal, and the Lyd Brook flowing quietly through the area.

Recreation:
The St. Regis River flows through the township. It provides great whitewater rafting and the DEC stocks the river yearly for good fishing.

There are also three lakes: Amber, Ozonia, and Jordan in our town. James Tharrett Park, a wooded area on the St. Regis River in Ft. Jackson has a picnic area.

There is good hunting and fishing in our town. There are also horseback trails and hiking on scenic routes. Maps are available for these trails.

Our two local stores are well supplied with fishing equipment, gas, camping supplies, foods and seated areas for lunches and coffee.

We would love your company! Please stop by and visit with us.

Material courtesy of Mary Converse, Hopkinton Town Historian

DATE: _____ WEATHER: _____

MEMORIES: _____

_____

_____

_____

_____

_____

_____

_____

_____

_____

_____

_____

_____

_____

_____

[Passport Stamp / Signature Here]

The Hopkinton Village Green located on Rt. 11B has many historic buildings. The Town Hall (off to the left) and the Congregation Church (to the left of the gazebo), were all placed on the New York Register of Historic Places in 2013. Mary Converse

LAWRENCE

The Town of Lawrence is in the eastern part of St. Lawrence County about halfway between Potsdam and Malone. It is named after William Lawrence, an early landowner. It contains these hamlets: Nicholville, Lawrenceville, and North Lawrence. The town is in the foothills of the Adirondacks with a small section of the Blue Line in the southern section on Port Kent Road.

The two rivers in this town are the Deere River flowing from the southeast to the northwest and the East Branch of the St. Regis River flowing across the southern part.

The two main roads going west to east are Rt. 11 and Rt. 11C. Another road is Rt. 11B traveling across the southeast section of town. It is also known as the Military Turnpike running from Plattsburg to Russell.

After 1800 settlers began arriving in the region, but during the War of 1812 many left permanently. When the state began constructing a road through the region in 1827 settlers began living in Lawrence again. In 1828 the Town of Lawrence was formed from parts of Hopkinton and Brasher. Farming and raising animals was the chief occupation.

Lawrenceville is the center of town. It had many stage coaches traveling through and the town had many thriving businesses. Many students from all over the North Country came to the Lawrenceville Academy, which was a top boarding school. There were many day students and the ones from far away lived on the third floor. The Lawrenceville Academy was razed in the 1950s and the Lawrenceville Fire Station now occupies that location.

During the early 1900s two fires devastated the town. Today most of the stores and the post office are gone. One of the church buildings is the home of the Paperback Browser & Peddlers Closet. There is a small park at the intersection of Rt. 11 and Co. Rt. 54. Its main purpose is as a memorial to our soldiers. The Town Municipal Complex, garages, and Town Museum are here. The museum is the home of the Lawrence Historical Organization. The Complex is just west of Lawrenceville on the north side of Rt. 11.

North Lawrence, in the northernmost part of town, was also a thriving community with two large hotels, feed store, milk factory, and many businesses. It was built by the railroad. Then a 1907 fire devastated the community. Today the major business is the milk factory. There is one restaurant, the Pit Stop, a grocery store, gas station, and TriTown Food Pantry all on Main St. (Rt. 11C).

There are six churches in our town. North Lawrence has a Roman Catholic Church and a Community Church. Lawrenceville has a Baptist Church. On Cemetery Road there is a Mennonite Church and Nicholville has a Catholic (not Roman) Church and a United Methodist Church.

At one time Nicholville was a roaring business community boasting a hotel, post office, pharmacy, its own doctor, and many stores. It was also a stopping place for stagecoaches heading towards Ogdensburg from Vermont. If you need food or gas there is Lucas Motor Sports/Twin Pines at 5 River St. in Nicholville. It is on the west side of the St. Regis by the intersection of Rts. 11B & 458.

Today the two main employers in town are the large milk plant in N. Lawrence and the Nicholville Telephone Co. the main dairy farm

DATE: _____ WEATHER: _____

MEMORIES: _____

_____

_____

_____

_____

_____

_____

_____

_____

_____

_____

_____

_____

_____

[Passport Stamp / Signature Here]

in Lawrence is Stauffers on Co. Rt. 54 just off Rt. 55. They are happy to give tours but you should call ahead. There are also many small farms that are run by the Amish who sell their farm products.

Material courtesy of Alice Stevenson, Town of Lawrence Historian

An Amish farm gathering hay. There are many Amish farms that sell vegetables and baked goods. St. Lawrence County Chamber of Commerce

PARISHVILLE

The Town of Parishville is in the south central part of St. Lawrence County. Part of the town is in the northwestern corner of the Adirondack Park. It is approx. 11 miles southeast of Potsdam. The town contains these hamlets: Parishville, Parishville Center, West Parishville, High Flats, and Pickettville.

The Parishville area was inhabited by the Mohawk Indian Tribe. On March 29, 1791 New York State made a treaty with the Mohawks, in which they surrendered title to their lands. The principle purchaser of this area was Alexander Macomb. The area was re-sold twice and then on Dec. 2, 1810 was purchased by David Parish, for whom the town is named.

There is a possibility that the Russell Turnpike, the present Colton Parishville Road, had already been cut and that Hoard's Rd. or path was connected with it. In 1810, Mr. Hoard enlarged this path into a road wide enough to permit horses and wagons for hauling building materials. In the meantime, the Town of Parishville had been surveyed and cut into lots.

The first settler was Luke Brown. He and several others came from Springfield, Vermont to work on the road. Mr. Parish let him choose land for a farm. In March, 1811, Brown brought his family to the farm located now on Rt. 72. They immediately tapped the nearest maple trees to begin sugaring since white sugar was very expensive.

The following March 30, 1812, the first child was born and christened Luke Parish Brown. Mr. Parish gave Luke 50 acres of land for his name. The official town of Parishville was formed March 18, 1814. It once had 14 mills located by the gorge in the hamlet of Parishville as well as several others outside but still in the town. The industrial era lasted only about 35 years.

We are very proud of our Parishville-Hopkinton Central School and our historic Town Hall, which is in very good condition and houses the Town Offices, located at 1067 White Hill Rd.

There are many sand and gravel businesses and logging is still operating throughout the area.

POINTS OF INTEREST

Sterling Pond and Joe Indian Pond are near the south town line. From the hamlet of Parrishville go south on White Hill Rd. and continue on Joe Indian Pond Rd.

Parishville Recreational Park is an outstanding park on the West Branch of the St. Regis River at 40 Park Rd. There is a beach for swimming, a nature trail, and playground facilities.

Parishville Museum is in the Bartlett mansion at 1785 Main St. It contains the history, artifacts, and archives of the town. Visitors are welcome July thru August, Tuesdays & Thursdays, 1 pm – 3 pm. www.parishvilleny.us/museum.htm

Services:
The Kunoco Food Mart with gas pumps and groceries is located at 1721 Rt. 72, in Parishville.

More information at www.parishvilleny.us.

Material courtesy of Joseph R. McGill, Town of Parishville Historian

DATE: _____ WEATHER: _____

MEMORIES: _____

_____

_____

_____

_____

_____

_____

_____

_____

_____

_____

_____

_____

_____

_____

_____

_____

[Passport Stamp / Signature Here]

Parishville Hamlet and Dam, Dam Built about 1924

A 1924 aerial view of the hamlet of Parishville (left) with Rt. 72 crossing over
the West Branch of the St. Regis River. A hydroelectric dam was built (c. 1924)
creating a pond. Allen Falls (near the lower bridge) is a popular attraction.
Joseph R. McGill

PIERCEFIELD

The Town of Piercefield is located in the southeastern corner of St. Lawrence County, approx. five miles west of Tupper Lake. It encompasses the hamlets of Childwold, Conifer, Gale, and Piercefield.

The hamlet of Piercefield, with its proximity to the Raquette River and Piercefield Falls, was the site of an International Paper Company pulp mill from 1899 to its closing in 1933. Piercefield was developed into a mill town, with company housing, stores, and public buildings.

The area's largest natural asset is the Raquette River. The 386-acre Raquette Flow can be accessed just west of the Rt. 3 bridge at Pumphouse Rd. There is a handicapped accessible dock and a boat launch offering good fishing and boating. There is a NYS lean-to on the south fork. Upstream from the flow, at Setting Pole Dam, there is a short portage which allows paddlers to access points upstream on the river.

The hamlet of Conifer was home to the Emporium Forestry Company for the first half of the 20th Century. The mill cut and processed hardwoods.

Massawepie was a fashionable resort hotel in Childwold that operated here from 1890-1909. It then became the private preserve of the Sykes family, who operated the Emporium Forestry Company and the related Grasse River Railroad in nearby Conifer and Cranberry Lake. The Boy Scouts purchased the property in 1951 for a summer camp.

POINTS OF INTEREST

Town of Piercefield Museum is located on Waller Street across from the Post Office.

Open from Memorial Day thru mid-October on Saturdays & Sundays, from 1 pm – 3 pm or by appointment by calling the Town Historian at 518-554-1001.

Childwold Memorial Presbyterian Church, (1893) a must-see historic church at 104 Bancroft Rd. It is open for services during the summer months. The church is listed on the National Register of Historic Places.

Leather Artisan offers more than 30 years of custom handcrafts including the highest domestic leathers, a wide variety of handbags, belts, men's and women's wallets and briefcases. 9740 Rt. 3, Childwold.

Camp Massawepie is a Boy Scout camp in the hamlet of Gale operated by the Seneca Waterways Council of the Boy Scouts of America. The camp is closed to the public when scouts are in residence during the summer.

Hikes:
Mt. Arab fire tower: It is a family friendly hike for all seasons. It can be accessed by turning on the road to Conifer from Rt. 3. It has a fire tower and observer's cabin restored by the Friends of Mt. Arab in 1997. There is a steward staffing the summit during the summer months.

Bog River Falls, Horseshoe Lake, and the Bog River: To get to these sites go south of the Village of Tupper Lake on Rt. 30. Turn right onto Rt. 421.

Material courtesy of Nancy Boeye, Town of Piercefield Historian

DATE: _____ WEATHER: _____

MEMORIES: _____

_____

_____

_____

_____

_____

_____

_____

_____

_____

_____

_____

_____

_____

_____

[Passport Stamp / Signature Here]

In 1899 International Paper Company construted this large pulp mill in Piercefield that made paper from the nearby forests. It was one of the largest mills in New England at the turn of the century, Piercefield developed into a mill town, with company housing, stores, and public buildings. The mill closed in 1933. Nancy Boeye

PITCARIN

The Town of Pitcairn is in the southwestern section of St. Lawrence County adjacent to the Village of Harrisville in Lewis County on the western border on Rt. 3. The southern part of the town is in the northwestern part of the Adirondack Park. The town includes these hamlets: Pitcairn (aka Pitcairn Forks), Geers Corners, Jayville, Kalurah, and East Pitcairn. The population of the town in 2010 was 846.

HISTORY

Settlers came to the eastern section of Pitcairn around 1824 when James Streeter began clearing the wilderness and the following year he brought his family. Other settlers followed and made small clearings and lived near Portaferry Lake. Gradually more settlers spread throughout the area.

On March 24, 1836 the town was established from parts of the towns of Fowler and Edwards. Daniel McCormick was assigned the town and he then transferred it to Joseph Pitcairn, who gave the town its name. There are many streams in the town and the dominant one is the Oswegatchie River. Most of the land is rough and rocky except for the narrow valleys where the land is productive.

The oldest standing house in Pitcairn is a stone house built by one of the very first settlers, Constant Wells, who came in 1824 and built the house in 1835. It is located along Co. Rt. 23 in the East Pitcairn area.

Camping, Hiking, Fishing, & Canoeing:
The town has hundreds of acres of State Land providing access to fishing streams, hiking trails, and canoeing. You can enjoy fishing on the Oswegatchie River or Jenny Creek.

Greenwood Creek State Forest is maintained by the DEC. It is accessible by driving about a mile along the Greenwood Road that is off Rt. 3 on the east side of Pitcairn. It has several trails maintained by the DEC. There is only a picnic area, but there are two camping sites along the road before you enter the parking lot. The forest was planted in 1935 by the Civilian Conservation Corps and today the 1.8-mile nature trail was built and maintained by the Star Lake Crew of the St. Lawrence County Youth Conservation Corps (YCC).

ATV Riding:
All roads in the Town of Pitcairn are open to ATV's with a main trail leading to Lewis County. There is also the Adirondack ATV Club that can be joined providing additional club trails for riding and use of their tracks and facilities. Camping on club grounds is also permitted for a small fee.

Snowmobiling:
There are several trails including main corridor trails leading to almost anywhere and to the Nice and Easy convenience store at the intersection of Rts. 812 & 3, Harrisville.

Lodging:
The Backwoods Retreat B&B provides off-the-beaten-path tourist accommodations. 241 Pinner Rd., off Rt. 812 going toward Gouverneur.

Material courtesy of Leland Ryan, Town of Pitcairn Historian

DATE: _____ WEATHER: _____

MEMORIES: _____

_____

_____

_____

_____

_____

_____

_____

_____

_____

_____

_____

_____

_____

_____

[Passport Stamp / Signature Here]

Stone House Built 1835 by Constant Wells

Constant Wells, one of the first settlers in Pitcairn, built this stone house in 1935. It is the oldest standing house in town and located along Co. Rt. 23 in East Pitcairn.
Leland Ryan

ACKNOWLEDGEMENTS

I would like to thank my wife, Lynn, for her encouragement and patience over the past year of research and writing; my children, Matthew, Kristy, and Ryan for their encouragement accompanying me on trips and hikes; my parents, Martin & Joan Podskoch; my son-in-law, Matthew Roloff, who helped me with computer problems; and my remarkable granddaughters, Kira and Lydia Roloff, for going on research trips with me.

A special thanks to Dr. Arthur W. Peach, who in a 1954 issue of Vermont Life magazine proposed an informal group to be known as the 251 Club after a reader asked him, "How can I come to know the real Vermont?" He invited local folk and newcomers alike to veer from the beaten path "to discover the secret and lovely places that the main roads do not reveal." He felt that all of Vermont had history, beauty, traditions, and interesting people. This is also true of the entire Adirondack region.

A special thank you to the following:

The approx. 100 writers for their time and effort to showcase their town or village.

My dedicated editor, David Hayden, who was always there to correct and guide me through the writing and editing of each town and village description. I never would have completed this book without his insightful questions and suggestions.

Retired District Ranger Paul Hartmann, who drew all of the maps for this book.

My sister-in-law, Sallie Way, for her logo design and passport idea.

Amanda Beauchemin for her excellent layout of this book and cover.

Barry Ford for his insights and encouragement.

Senator Betty Little for her dedication and hard work for her Adirondack constituents and for her insightful Preface for this book.

Jeri Wright for her timely and beautiful cover photo.

Without the encouragement of the Adirondack Association of Towns & Villages (AATV), its member Clark Seaman Supervisor of Long Lake, AATV President Brian Towers, and AATV Secretary Carol Hart, the seed for the Adirondack 102 Club would still lie dormant in my brain. Their encouragement and the AATV supervisors, mayors, and their staffs helped make the club and book a reality.

Thanks to these local and regional Chambers of Commerce which provided town and village descriptions and photos: Elizabethtown-Lewis, Moriah, Westport, and Kathy Van Anden of Saranac Lake. Also, thanks to Kimberly Rielly, the Director of Communications for the Lake Placid Convention and Visitors Bureau/Regional Office of Sustainable Tourism.

Thank you to the following people, businesses, and organizations that supplied photos for the book and website: Lynn Benevento, Vicky Roy, Carolyn and Gene Ouderkirk, John Davie, Don Mauer, Mike Farrell, Dave Petrelli, Allison M. Richards, Kimberly Woods, Margaret Bartley, Bob Lilly, Laurent Inard, Carol Murtagh & Paul Lemieux, Loretta Ransom, Dave McGrath, Doug Seig, Maureen Lanfear, Joe Hammecker Lapland Lake Nordic Center, Jill Jones of Bloated Toe Publishing, Tammi Subik of Saltsmans Hotel, Paige Doerner of the Adirondack Museum, Kristy Graham and Gail Murray of the Town of Webb Historical Association, the Woodgate Library, Wilmington Historical Society, Ticonderoga Heritage Museum, Warren County Historical Society, Regional Office of Sustainable Tourism, Warrensburg Historical Society, Hague Historical Society, Tim Bresett of Chasm Falls, Mary McGowan Administrative Director of Meadowmount School of Music, Lucinda Smarro of the Beaversprite Nature Center, Debbie Abbott-Forgione of Alicia Miller Real Estate, Vincent Cangelosi, Joan Rock of The Log Chapel, Marlene Almodovar of North Country Underground Railroad Museum, Doreen Ossenkop of Adirondack Buffalo Farm, NYSDEC, Margo Kourofsky of Friends of Lyon Mountain Mining and Railroad Museum, the NYS Office of Parks, Recreation & Historic Preservation, and Warren County Tourism.

INDEX

ABOUT THE AUTHOR

Marty Podskoch was a reading teacher for 28 years at Delaware Academy in Delhi, NY. He retired in 2001. Marty and his wife, Lynn, raised their three children, Matt, Kristy, and Ryan, in a renovated 19th c. farmhouse along the West Branch of the Delaware River. He became interested in fire towers after climbing to the fire tower on Hunter Mountain in the fall of 1987. He met the observer, who was in his 60s, chatted with him, and listened to his stories. Marty was hooked. He set out on a quest to find out all he could about the history and lore of the fire towers.

In 1997 Wray Rominger of Purple Mountain Press asked Marty to write about the history of the Catskill fire towers and the restoration project that was occurring in the Catskills.

After interviewing over 100 observers, rangers, and their families, Marty had gathered hundreds of stories and pictures about the 23 fire towers in the Catskill region. In 2000 his book, Fire Towers of the Catskills: Their History and Lore, was published by Purple Mountain Press, which also published his second book, Adirondack Fire Towers: Their History and Lore, the Southern Districts, in June of 2003 and his third title, Adirondack Fire Towers: Their History and Lore, the Northern Districts, in November of 2005.

Marty also wrote a weekly newspaper column, "Adirondack Stories" in five area newspapers. Sam Glanzman, a noted comic book illustrator for the past 50 years, illustrated the stories. After five years of weekly columns Podskoch Press published 251 illustrated stories in two volumes: Adirondack Stories: Historical Sketches and Adirondack Stories II: 101 More Historical Sketches.

In 20011 Podskoch wrote and published: Adirondack Civilian Conservation Corps Camps: History, Memories & Legacy of the CCC. Presently he is doing research on the Civilian Conservation Corps camps in Connecticut and Rhode Island.

In the fall of 2013 Podskoch received the "Arthur E. Newkirk Education Award" from the Adirondack Mountain Club for his work in preserving the history of the fire towers and Civilian Conservation Corps Camps in the Adirondacks and Catskills.

Marty Podskoch and family at his lake house in East Hampton, CT. Front row: Lydia & Kira Roloff and dog, "Tank." Second row: son Ryan, wife, Lynn, daughter, Kristy Roloff, and Marty. Third row: Matt Podskoch and Matt Roloff.